. . .

EMILY DICKINSON

COLLECTED POEMS

COURAGE
BOOKS

an imprint of
RUNNING PRESS
Philadelphia, Pennsylvania

The essay "Emily Dickinson and the Poetry of the Inner Life" by Elizabeth
Jennings is an excerpt from the essay published in *A Review of English
Literature,* Volume Three, Number Two (April, 1962), © 1962 Longmans,
Green and Co., Inc. and is reprinted by permission of The University of
Calgary Press.

"Emily Dickinson" from *American Characteristics* by Thornton Wilder. © 1957
by Thornton Wilder. Reprinted by permission of HarperCollins Publishers.

Canadian representatives: General Publishing Co., Ltd., 30 Lesmill Road,
Don Mills, Ontario M3B 2T6.

International representatives: Worldwide Media Services, Inc., 115 East
Twenty-third Street, New York, New York 10010.

9 8 7 6 5 4 3
Digit on the right indicates the number of this printing.

Library of Congress Cataloging-in-publication Number 91-71089

ISBN 1-56138-045-8

Editor: Peter Siegenthaler
Jacket design by Toby Schmidt
Interior design by Nancy Loggins
Typography: ITC Berkeley Oldstyle, by Commcor
Communications Corporation, Philadelphia, Pennsylvania

Published by Courage Books, an imprint of
Running Press Book Publishers
125 South Twenty-second Street
Philadelphia, Pennsylvania 19103

Contents

Contents

. . .

INTRODUCTION

NOW celebrated as one of America's greatest poets, Emily
Dickinson is also famous for her quiet, private life. The
daughter of a prominent lawyer and Congressman of Amherst,
Massachusetts, she confined her activities to the grounds of the
family home. She traveled out of Amherst only a handful of
times, and did not marry. Later in her life she dressed all in
white and acquired a reputation as an eccentric recluse.

In her self-imposed isolation, Dickinson's passion and
perception found outlet in poetry of dazzling honesty and
originality. Although she corresponded with the essayist and
critic Thomas Wentworth Higginson and often accompanied
gifts to family and friends with snippets of verse, no one
realized the scope of her writing until after her death in 1886.
The subsequent publication and appreciation of her work are a
testament to the fruitfulness of her solitary labors.

This edition gathers the first four volumes of Dickinson's
poetry, complete with their introductions and preludes. We have
endeavored to let the poems speak for themselves, and in this
spirit we have deleted titles added by Dickinson's original
editors, titles not envisioned by the poet herself. Otherwise, the
poems appear here just as they did upon first publication.

In the century since the first of these books introduced her
verse to the public, Emily Dickinson has become one of the
world's best-loved writers. Her poems continue to offer their
unflinching exploration of the human condition and a tender
appreciation of nature and love.

. . .

POEMS

BY

EMILY DICKINSON

. . .

P RELUDE

This is my letter to the world,
  That never wrote to me,–
The simple news that Nature told,
  With tender majesty.

Her message is committed
  To hands I cannot see;
For love of her, sweet countrymen,
  Judge tenderly of me!

. . .

Preface

THE verses of Emily Dickinson belong emphatically to what Emerson long since called "the Poetry of the Portfolio" – something produced absolutely without the thought of publication, and solely by way of expression of the writer's own mind. Such verse must inevitably forfeit whatever advantage lies in the discipline of public criticism and the enforced conformity to accepted ways. On the other hand, it may often gain something through the habit of freedom and the unconventional utterance of daring thoughts. In the case of the present author, there was absolutely no choice in the matter; she must write thus, or not at all. A recluse by temperament and habit, literally spending years without setting her foot beyond the doorstep, and many more years during which her walks were strictly limited to her father's grounds, she habitually concealed her mind, like her person, from all but a very few friends; and it was with great difficulty that she was persuaded to print, during her lifetime, three or four poems. Yet she wrote verses in great abundance; and though curiously indifferent to all conventional rules, had yet a rigorous literary standard of her own, and often altered a word many times to suit an ear which had its own tenacious fastidiousness.

Miss Dickinson was born in Amherst, Mass., Dec. 10, 1830, and died there May 15, 1886. Her father, Hon. Edward Dickinson, was the leading lawyer of Amherst, and was treasurer of the well-known college there situated. It was his custom once a year to hold a large reception at his house, attended by all the families connected with the institution and by the leading people of the town. On these occasions his daughter Emily emerged from her wonted retirement and did her part as gracious hostess; nor would any one have known from her manner, I have been told, that this was not a daily occurrence. The annual occasion once past, she withdrew again into her seclusion, and except for a very few friends was as invisible to the world as if she had dwelt in a nunnery. For myself, although I had corresponded with her for many years, I saw her but twice face to face, and brought away the impression of something as unique and remote as Undine or Mignon or Thekla.

This selection from her poems is published to meet the desire of her personal friends, and especially of her surviving sister. It is believed that the thoughtful reader will find in these pages a quality more suggestive of the poetry of William Blake than of anything to be elsewhere found,—flashes of wholly original and profound insight into nature and life; words and phrases exhibiting an extraordinary vividness of descriptive and imaginative power, yet often set in a seemingly whimsical or even rugged frame. They are here published as they were written, with very few and superficial changes. In many cases these verses will seem to the reader like poetry torn up by the roots, with rain and dew and earth still clinging to them, giving a freshness and a fragrance not otherwise to be conveyed. In other cases, as in the few poems of shipwreck or of mental conflict, we can only wonder at the gift of vivid imagination by which this recluse woman can delineate, by a few touches, the very crises of physical or mental struggle. And sometimes again we catch glimpses of a lyric strain, sustained perhaps but for a line or two at a time, and making the reader regret its sudden cessation. But the main quality of these poems is that of extraordinary grasp and insight, uttered with an uneven vigor sometimes exasperating, seemingly wayward, but really unsought and inevitable. After all, when a thought takes one's breath away, a lesson on grammar seems an impertinence. As

Ruskin wrote in his earlier and better days, "No weight nor mass nor beauty of execution can outweigh one grain or fragment of thought."

THOMAS WENTWORTH HIGGINSON

I. LIFE

I.

SUCCESS is counted sweetest
       By those who ne'er succeed.
To comprehend a nectar
Requires sorest need.

Not one of all the purple host
Who took the flag to-day
Can tell the definition,
So clear, of victory,

As he, defeated, dying,
On whose forbidden ear
The distant strains of triumph
Break, agonized and clear.

II.

OUR share of night to bear,
       Our share of morning,
Our blank in bliss to fill,
Our blank in scorning.

Here a star, and there a star,
Some lose their way.
Here a mist, and there a mist,
Afterwards—day!

III.

SOUL, wilt thou toss again?
        By just such a hazard
Hundreds have lost, indeed,
But tens have won an all.

Angels' breathless ballot
Lingers to record thee;
Imps in eager caucus
Raffle for my soul

IV.

'TIS so much joy! 'T is so much joy!
        If I should fail, what poverty!
And yet, as poor as I
Have ventured all upon a throw;
Have gained! Yes! Hesitated so
This side the victory!

Life is but life, and death but death!
Bliss is but bliss, and breath but breath!
And if, indeed, I fail,
At least to know the worst is sweet.
Defeat means nothing but defeat,
No drearier can prevail!

And if I gain,—oh, gun at sea,
Oh, bells that in the steeples be,
At first repeat it slow!
For heaven is a different thing
Conjectured, and waked sudden in,
And might o'erwhelm me so!

V.

GLEE! the great storm is over!
    Four have recovered the land;
Forty gone down together
Into the boiling sand.

Ring, for the scant salvation!
Toll, for the bonnie souls,–
Neighbor and friend and bridegroom,
Spinning upon the shoals!

How they will tell the shipwreck
When winter shakes the door,
Till the children ask, "But the forty?
Did they come back no more?"

Then a silence suffuses the story,
And a softness the teller's eye;
And the children no further question,
And only the waves reply.

VI.

IF I can stop one heart from breaking,
    I shall not live in vain;
If I can ease one life the aching,
Or cool one pain,
Or help one fainting robin
Unto his nest again,
I shall not live in vain.

VII.

WITHIN my reach!
        I could have touched!
I might have chanced that way!
Soft sauntered through the village,
Sauntered as soft away!
So unsuspected violets
Within the fields lie low,
Too late for striving fingers
That passed, an hour ago.

VIII.

A WOUNDED deer leaps highest,
        I've heard the hunter tell;
'Tis but the ecstasy of death,
And then the brake is still.

The smitten rock that gushes,
The trampled steel that springs:
A cheek is always redder
Just where the hectic stings!

Mirth is the mail of anguish,
In which it cautious arm,
Lest anybody spy the blood
And "You're hurt" exclaim!

IX.

THE heart asks pleasure first,
        And then, excuse from pain;
And then, those little anodynes
That deaden suffering;

And then, to go to sleep;
And then, if it should be
The will of its Inquisitor,
The liberty to die.

X.

A PRECIOUS, mouldering pleasure 't is
        To meet an antique book,
In just the dress his century wore;
A privilege, I think,

His venerable hand to take,
And warming in our own,
A passage back, or two, to make
To times when he was young.

His quaint opinions to inspect,
His knowledge to unfold
On what concerns our mutual mind,
The literature of old;

What interested scholars most,
What competitions ran
When Plato was a certainty,
And Sophocles a man;

When Sappho was a living girl,
And Beatrice wore
The gown that Dante deified.
Facts, centuries before,

He traverses familiar,
As one should come to town
And tell you all your dreams were true:
He lived where dreams were sown.

His presence is enchantment,
You beg him not to go;
Old volumes shake their vellum heads
And tantalize, just so.

XI.

MUCH madness is divinest sense
        To a discerning eye;
Much sense the starkest madness.
'T is the majority
In this, as all, prevails.
Assent, and you are sane;
Demur,—you're straightway dangerous,
And handled with a chain.

XII.

I ASKED no other thing,
        No other was denied.
I offered Being for it;
The mighty merchant smiled.

Brazil? He twirled a button,
Without a glance my way:
"But madam, is there nothing else
That we can show to-day?"

XIII.

THE soul selects her own society,
        Then shuts the door;
On her divine majority
Obtrude no more.

Unmoved, she notes the chariot's pausing
At her low gate;
Unmoved, an emperor is kneeling
Upon her mat.

I've known her from an ample nation
Choose one;
Then close the valves of her attention
Like stone.

XIV.

SOME things that fly there be,–
        Birds, hours, the bumble-bee:
Of these no elegy.

Some things that stay there be,–
Grief, hills, eternity:
Nor this behooveth me.

There are, that resting, rise.
Can I expound the skies?
How still the riddle lies!

XV.

I KNOW some lonely houses off the road
        A robber'd like the look of,–
Wooden barred,
And windows hanging low,
Inviting to
A portico,
Where two could creep:
One hand the tools,
The other peep
To make sure all's asleep.
Old-fashioned eyes,
Not easy to surprise!

How orderly the kitchen'd look by night,
With just a clock,–
But they could gag the tick,
And mice won't bark;
And so the walls don't tell, None will.
A pair of spectacles ajar just stir –
An almanac's aware.
Was it the mat winked,
Or a nervous star?
The moon slides down the stair
To see who's there.

There's plunder,–where?
Tankard, or spoon,
Earring, or stone,
A watch, some ancient brooch
To match the grandmamma,
Staid sleeping there.

Day-rattles, too,
Stealth's slow;
The sun has got as far
As the third sycamore.
Screams chanticleer,
"Who's there?"
Sneer–"Where?"
While the old couple, just astir,
Fancy the sunrise left the door ajar!

XVI.

TO fight aloud is very brave,
    But gallanter, I know,
Who charge within the bosom,
The cavalry of woe.

Who win, and nations do not see,
Who fall, and none observe,
Whose dying eyes no country
Regards with patriot love.

We trust, in plumed procession,
For such the angels go,
Rank after rank, with even feet
And uniforms of snow.

XVII.

WHEN night is almost done,
    And sunrise grows so near
That we can touch the spaces,
It's time to smooth the hair.

And get the dimples ready,
And wonder we could care
For that old faded midnight
That frightened but an hour.

XVIII.

READ, sweet, how others strove,
 Till we are stouter;
What they renounced,
Till we are less afraid;
How many times they bore
The faithful witness,
Till we are helped,
As if a kingdom cared!

Read then of faith
That shone above the fagot;
Clear strains of hymn
The river could not drown;
Brave names of men
And celestial women,
Passed out of record
Into renown!

XIX.

PAIN has an element of blank;
 It cannot recollect
When it began, or if there were
A day when it was not.

It has no future but itself,
Its infinite realms contain
Its past, enlightened to perceive
New periods of pain.

XX.

I TASTE a liquor never brewed,
        From tankards scooped in pearl;
Not all the vats upon the Rhine
Yield such an alcohol!

Inebriate of air am I,
And debauchee of dew,
Reeling, through endless summer days,
From inns of molten blue.

When landlords turn the drunken bee
Out of the foxglove's door,
When butterflies renounce their drams,
I shall but drink the more!

Till seraphs swing their snowy hats,
And saints to windows run,
To see the little tippler
Leaning against the sun!

XXI.

HE ate and drank the precious words,
        His spirit grew robust;
He knew no more that he was poor,
Nor that his frame was dust.
He danced along the dingy days,
And this bequest of wings
Was but a book. What liberty
A loosened spirit brings!

XXII.

I HAD no time to hate, because
      The grave would hinder me,
And life was not so ample I
Could finish enmity.

Nor had I time to love; but since
Some industry must be,
The little toil of love, I thought,
Was large enough for me.

XXIII.

'T WAS such a little, little boat
      That toddled down the bay!
'T was such a gallant, gallant sea
That beckoned it away!

'T was such a greedy, greedy wave
That licked it from the coast;
Nor ever guessed the stately sails
My little craft was lost!

XXIV.

WHETHER my bark went down at sea,
    Whether she met with gales,
Whether to isles enchanted
She bent her docile sails;

By what mystic mooring
She is held to-day,—
This is the errand of the eye
Out upon the bay.

XXV.

BELSHAZZAR had a letter,—
    He never had but one;
Belshazzar's correspondent
Concluded and begun
In that immortal copy
The conscience of us all
Can read without its glasses
On revelation's wall.

XXVI.

THE brain within its groove
    Runs evenly and true;
But let a splinter swerve,
'T were easier for you
To put the water back
When floods have slit the hills,
And scooped a turnpike for themselves,
And blotted out the mills!

II. LOVE

I.

MINE by the right of the white election!
        Mine by the royal seal!
Mine by the sign in the scarlet prison
Bars cannot conceal!

Mine, here in vision and in veto!
Mine, by the grave's repeal
Titled, confirmed,—delirious charter!
Mine, while the ages steal!

II.

YOU left me, sweet, two legacies,—
        A legacy of love
A Heavenly Father would content,
Had He the offer of;

You left me boundaries of pain
Capacious as the sea,
Between eternity and time,
Your consciousness and me.

III.

ALTER? When the hills do.
      Falter? When the sun
Question if his glory
Be the perfect one.

Surfeit? When the daffodil
Doth of the dew:
Even as herself, O friend!
I will of you!

IV.

ELYSIUM is as far as to
      The very nearest room,
If in that room a friend await
Felicity or doom.

What fortitude the soul contains,
That it can so endure
The accent of a coming foot,
The opening of a door!

V.

DOUBT me, my dim companion!
    Why, God would be content
With but a fraction of the love
Poured thee without a stint.
The whole of me, forever,
What more the woman can,—
Say quick, that I may dower thee
With last delight I own!

It cannot be my spirit,
For that was thine before;
I ceded all of dust I knew,—
What opulence the more
Had I, a humble maiden,
Whose farthest of degree
Was that she might,
Some distant heaven,
Dwell timidly with thee!

VI.

IF you were coming in the fall,
    I'd brush the summer by
With half a smile and half a spurn,
As housewives do a fly.

If I could see you in a year,
I'd wind the months in balls,
And put them each in separate drawers,
Until their time befalls.

If only centuries delayed,
I'd count them on my hand,
Subtracting till my fingers dropped
Into Van Diemen's land.

If certain, when this life was out,
That yours and mine should be,
I'd toss it yonder like a rind,
And taste eternity.

But now, all ignorant of the length
Of time's uncertain wing,
It goads me, like the goblin bee,
That will not state its sting.

VII.

I HIDE myself within my flower,
          That wearing on your breast,
You, unsuspecting, wear me too —
And angels know the rest.

I hide myself within my flower,
That, fading from your vase,
You, unsuspecting, feel for me
Almost a loneliness.

VIII.

THAT I did always love,
    I bring thee proof:
That till I loved
I did not love enough.

That I shall love alway,
I offer thee
That love is life,
And life hath immorality.

This, dost thou doubt, sweet?
Then have I
Nothing to show
But Calvary.

IX.

HAVE you got a brook in your little heart,
    Where bashful flowers blow,
And blushing birds go down to drink,
And shadows tremble so?

And nobody knows, so still it flows,
That any brook is there;
And yet your little draught of life
Is daily drunken there.

Then look out for the little brook in March,
When the rivers overflow,
And the snows come hurrying from the hills,
And the bridges often go.

And later, in August it may be,
When the meadows parching lie,
Beware, lest this little brook of life
Some burning noon go dry!

X.

AS if some little Arctic flower,
        Upon the polar hem,
Went wandering down the latitudes,
Until it puzzled came
To continents of summer,
To firmaments of sun,
To strange, bright crowds of flowers,
And birds of foreign tongue!
I say, as if this little flower
To Eden wandered in –
What then? Why, nothing, only
Your inference therefrom!

XI.

MY river runs to thee:
     Blue sea, wilt
welcome me?

My river waits reply.
Oh, sea, look graciously!

I'll fetch thee brooks
From spotted nooks,–

Say, sea,
Take me!

XII.

I CANNOT live with you,
      It would be life,
And life is over there
Behind the shelf

The sexton keeps the key to,
Putting up
Our life, his porcelain,
Like a cup

Discarded of the housewife,
Quaint or broken;
A newer Sèvres pleases,
Old ones crack.

I could not die with you,
For one must wait
To shut the other's gaze down,–
You could not.

And I, could I stand by
And see you freeze,
Without my right of frost,
Death's privilege?

Nor could I rise with you,
Because your face
Would put out Jesus',
That new grace

Glow-plain and foreign
On my homesick eye,
Except that you, than he
Shone closer by.

They'd judge us – how?
For you served Heaven, you know,
Or sought to;
I could not,

Because you saturated sight,
And I had no more eyes
For sordid excellence
As Paradise.

And were you lost, I would be,
Though my name
Rang loudest
On the heavenly fame.

And were you saved,
And I condemned to be
Where you were not,
That self were hell to me.

So we must keep apart,
You there, I here,
With just the door ajar
That oceans are,
And prayer,
And that pale sustenance,
Despair!

XIII.

THERE came a day at summer's full
Entirely for me;
I thought that such were for the saints,
Where revelations be.

The sun, as common, went abroad,
The flowers, accustomed, blew,
As if no soul the solstice passed
That maketh all things new.

The time was scarce profaned by speech;
The symbol of a word
Was needless, as at sacrament
The wardrobe of our Lord.

Each was to each the sealed church,
Permitted to commune this time,
Lest we too awkward show
At supper of the Lamb.

The hours slid fast, as hours will,
Clutched tight by greedy hands;
So faces on two decks look back,
Bound to opposing lands.

And so, when all the time had failed,
Without external sound,
Each bound the other's crucifix,
We gave no other bond.

Sufficient troth that we shall rise –
Deposed, at length, the grave –
To that new marriage, justified
Through Calvaries of Love!

XIV.

I'M ceded, I've stopped being theirs;
        The name they dropped upon my face
With water, in the country church,
Is finished using now,
And they can put it with my dolls,
My childhood, and the string of spools
I've finished threading too.

Baptized before without the choice,
But this time consciously, of grace
Unto supremest name,
Called to my full, the crescent dropped,
Existence's whole arc filled up
With one small diadem.

My second rank, too small the first,
Crowned, crowing on my father's breast,
A half unconscious queen;
But this time, adequate, erect,
With will to choose or to reject,
And I choose—just a throne.

XV.

'TWAS a long parting, but the time
        For interview had come;
Before the judgment-seat of God,
The last and second time

These fleshless lovers met,
A heaven in a gaze,
A heaven of heavens, the privilege
On one another's eyes.

No lifetime set on them,
Apparelled as the new
Unborn, except they had beheld,
Born everlasting now.

Was bridal e'er like this?
A paradise, the host,
A cherubim and seraphim
The most familiar guest.

XVI.

I'M wife; I've finished that,
        That other state;
I'm Czar, I'm woman now:
It's safer so.

How odd the girl's life looks
Behind this soft eclipse!
I think that earth seems so
To those in heaven now.

This being comfort, then
That other kind was pain;
But why compare?
I'm wife! stop there!

XVII.

SHE rose to his requirement, dropped
         The playthings of her life
To take the honorable work
Of woman and of wife.

If aught she missed in her new day
Of amplitude, or awe,
Or first prospective, or the gold
In using wore away,

It lay unmentioned, as the sea
Develops pearl and weed,
But only to himself is known
The fathoms they abide.

XVIII.

COME slowly, Eden!
         Lips unused to thee,
Bashful, sip thy jasmines,
As the fainting bee,

Reaching late his flower,
Round her chamber hums,
Counts his nectars—enters,
And is lost in balms!

III. Nature

I.

NEW feet within my garden go,
        New fingers stir the sod;
A troubadour upon the elm
Betrays the solitude.

New children play upon the green,
New weary sleep below;
And still the pensive spring returns,
And still the punctual snow!

II.

PINK, small, and punctual,
        Aromatic, low,
Covert in April,
Candid in May,

Dear to the moss,
Known by the knoll,
Next to the robin
In every human soul.

Bold little beauty,
Bedecked with thee,
Nature forswears
Antiquity.

III.

THE murmur of a bee
        A witchcraft yieldeth me.
If any ask me why,
'T were easier to die
Than tell.

The red upon the hill
Taketh away my will;
If anybody sneer,
Take care, for God is here,
That's all.

The breaking of the day
Addeth to my degree;
If any ask me how,
Artist, who drew me so,
Must tell!

IV.

PERHAPS you'd like to buy a flower?
        But I could never sell.
If you would like to borrow
Until the daffodil

Unties her yellow bonnet
Beneath the village door,
Until the bees, from clover rows
Their hock and sherry draw,

Why, I will lend until just then,
But not an hour more!

V.

THE pedigree of honey
     Does not concern the bee;
A clover, any time, to him
Is aristocracy.

VI.

SOME keep the Sabbath going to church;
     I keep it staying at home,
With bobolink for a chorister,
And an orchard for a dome.

Some keep the Sabbath in surplice;
I just wear my wings,
And instead of tolling the bell for church,
Our little sexton sings.

God preaches,—a noted clergyman,—
And the sermon is never long;
So instead of getting to heaven at last,
I'm going all along!

VII.

THE bee is not afraid of me,
    I know the butterfly;
The pretty people in the woods
Receive me cordially.

The brooks laugh louder when I come,
The breezes madder play.
Wherefore, mine eyes, they silver mists?
Wherefore, O summer's day?

VIII.

SOME rainbow coming from the fair!
         Some vision of the world Cashmere
I confidently see!
Or else a peacock's purple train,
Feather by feather, on the plain
Fritters itself away!

The dreamy butterflies bestir,
Lethargic pools resume the whir
Of last year's sundered tune.
From some old fortress on the sun
Baronial bees march, one by one,
In murmuring platoon!

The robins stand as thick today
As flakes of snow stood yesterday,
On fence and roof and twig.
The orchis binds her feather on
For her old lover, Don the Sun,
Revisiting the bog!

Without commander, countless, still,
The regiment of wood and hill
In bright detachment stand.
Behold! Whose multitudes are these?
The children of whose turbaned seas,
Or what Circassian land?

IX.

THE grass so little has to do,–
    A sphere of simple green,
With only butterflies to brood,
And bees to entertain,

And stir all day to pretty tunes
The breezes fetch along,
And hold the sunshine in its lap
And bow to everything;

And thread the dews all night, like pearls,
And make itself so fine,–
A duchess were too common
For such a noticing.

And even when it dies, to pass
In odors so divine,
As lowly spices gone to sleep,
Or amulets of pine.

And then to dwell in sovereign barns,
And dream the days away,–
The grass so little has to do,
I wish I were the hay!

X.

A LITTLE road not made of man,
         Enabled of the eye,
Accessible to thill of bee,
Or cart of butterfly.

If town it have, beyond itself,
'T is that I cannot say;
I only sigh,—no vehicle
Bears me along that way.

XI.

A DROP fell on the apple tree,
         Another on the roof;
A half a dozen kissed the eaves,
And made the gables laugh.

A few went out to help the brook,
That went to help the sea.
Myself conjectured, Were they pearls,
What necklaces could be!

The dust replaced in hoisted roads,
The birds jocoser sung;
The sunshine threw his hat away,
The orchards spangles hung.

The breezes brought dejected lutes,
And bathed them in the glee;
The East put out a single flag,
And signed the fête away.

XII.

A SOMETHING in a summer's day,
      As slow her flambeaux burn away,
Which solemnizes me.

A something in a summer's noon,–
An azure depth, a wordless tune,
Transcending ecstasy.

And still within a summer's night
A something so transporting bright,
I clap my hands to see;

The veil my too inspecting face,
Lest such a subtle, shimmering grace
Flutter too far for me.

The wizard-fingers never rest,
The purple brook within the breast
Still chafes its narrow bed;

Still rears the East her amber flag,
Guides still the sun along the crag
His caravan of red,

Like flowers that heard the tale of dews,
But never deemed the dripping prize
Awaited their low brows;

Or bees, that thought the summer's name
Some rumor of delirium
No summer could for them;

Or Arctic creature, dimly stirred
By tropic hint,—some travelled bird
Imported to the wood;

Or wind's bright signal to the ear,
Making that homely and severe,
Contented, known, before

The heaven unexpected came,
To lives that thought their worshiping
A too presumptuous psalm.

XIII.

THIS is the land the sunset washes,
      These are the banks of the Yellow Sea;
Where it rose, or whither it rushes,
These are the western mystery!

Night after night her purple traffic
Strews the landing with opal bales;
Merchantmen poise upon horizons,
Dip, and vanish with fairy sails.

XIV.

THERE is a flower that bees prefer,
    And butterflies desire;
To gain the purple democrat
The hummingbirds aspire.

And whatsoever insect pass,
A honey bears away
Proportioned to his several dearth
And her capacity.

Her face is rounder than the moon,
And ruddier than the gown
Of orchis in the pasture,
Or rhododendron worn.

She doth not wait for June;
Before the world is green
Her sturdy little countenance
Against the wind is seen,

Contending with the grass,
Near kinsman to herself,
For privilege of sod and sun,
Sweet litigants for life.

And when the hills are full, and newer fashions blow,
Doth not retract a single spice
For pang of jealousy.

Her public is the noon,
Her providence the sun,
Her progress by the bee proclaimed
In sovereign, swerveless tune.

The bravest of the host,
Surrendering the last,
Nor even of defeat aware
When cancelled by the frost.

XV.

L IKE trains of cars on tracks of plush
        I hear the level bee:
A jar across the flowers goes,
Their velvet masonry

Withstands until the sweet assault
Their chivalry consumes,
While he, victorious, tilts away
To vanquish other blooms.

His feet are shod with gauze,
His helmet is of gold;
His breast, a single onyx
With chrysoprase, inlaid.

His labor is a chant,
His idleness a tune;
Oh, for a bee's experience
Of clovers and of noon!

XVI.

PRESENTIMENT is that long shadow on the lawn
        Indicative that suns go down;
The notice to the startled grass
That darkness is about to pass.

XVII.

AS children bid the guest good-night,
        And then reluctant turn,
My flowers raise their pretty lips,
Then put their nightgowns on.

As children caper when they wake,
Merry that it is morn,
My flowers from a hundred cribs
Will peep, and prance again.

XVIII.

ANGELS in the early morning
        May be seen the dews among,
Stooping, plucking, smiling, flying:
Do the buds to them belong?

Angels when the sun is hottest
May be seen the sands among,
Stooping, plucking, sighing, flying;
Parched the flowers they bear along.

XIX.

SO bashful when I spied her,
      So pretty, so ashamed!
So hidden in her leaflets,
Lest anybody find;

So breathless till I passed her,
So helpless when I turned
And bore her, struggling, blushing,
Her simple haunts beyond!

For whom I robbed the dingle,
For whom betrayed the dell,
Many will doubtless ask me,
But I shall never tell!

XX.

IT makes no difference abroad,
      The seasons fit the same,
The mornings blossom into noons,
And split their pods of flame.

Wild-flowers kindle in the woods,
The brooks brag all the day;
No blackbird bates his jargoning
For passing Calvary.

Auto-da-fé and judgment
Are nothing to the bee;
His separation from the rose
To him seems misery.

XXI.

THE mountain sat upon the plain
        In his eternal chair,
His observation omnifold,
His inquest everywhere.

The seasons prayed around his knees,
Like children round a sire:
Grandfather of the days is he,
Of dawn the ancestor.

XXII.

I'LL tell you how the sun rose,—
        A ribbon at a time.
The steeples swam in amethyst,
The news like squirrels ran.
                    •
The hills untied their bonnets,
The bobolinks begun.
Then I said softly to myself,
"That must have been the sun!"
        •   •   •   •   •   •
But how he set, I know not.
There seemed a purple stile
Which little yellow boys and girls
Were climbing all the while

Till when they reached the other side,
A dominie in gray
Put gently up the evening bars,
And led the flock away.

XXIII.

THE butterfly's assumption-gown,
        In chrysoprase apartments hung,
This afternoon put on.

How condescending to descend,
And be of buttercups the friend
    In a New England town!

XXIV.

OF all the sounds despatched abroad,
        There's not a charge to me
Like that old measure in the boughs,
That phraseless melody

The wind does, working like a hand
Whose fingers brush the sky,
Then quiver down, with tufts of tune
Permitted gods and me.

When winds go round and round in bands,
And thrum upon the door,
And birds take places overhead,
To bear them orchestra,

I crave him grace, of summer boughs,
If such an outcast be,
He never heard that fleshless chant
Rise solemn in the tree,

As if some caravan of sound
On deserts, in the sky,
Had broken rank,
Then knit, and passed
In seamless company.

XXV.

APPARENTLY with no surprise
    To any happy flower,
The frost beheads it at its play
In accidental power.
The blond assassin passes on,
The sun proceeds unmoved
To measure off another day
For an approving God.

XXVI.

'T WAS later when the summer went
    Than when the cricket came,
And yet we knew that gentle clock
Meant nought but going home.

'T was sooner when the cricket went
Than when the winter came,
Yet that pathetic pendulum
Keeps esoteric time.

XXVII.

THESE are the days when birds come back,
    A very few, a bird or two,
To take a backward look.

These are the days when skies put on
The old, old sophistries of June,—
A blue and gold mistake.

Oh, fraud that cannot cheat the bee,
Almost thy plausibility
Induces my belief,

Till ranks of seeds their witness bear,
And softly through the altered air
Hurries a timid leaf!

Oh, sacrament of summer days,
Oh, last communion in the haze,
Permit a child to join,

Thy sacred emblems to partake,
Thy consecrated bread to break,
Taste thine immortal wine!

XXVIII.

THE morns are meeker than they were,
      The nuts are getting brown;
The berry's cheek is plumper,
The rose is out of town.

The maple wears a gayer scarf,
The field a scarlet gown.
Lest I should be old-fashioned,
I'll put a trinket on.

XXIX.

THE sky is low, the clouds are mean,
      A travelling flake of snow
Across a barn or through a rut
Debates if it will go.

A narrow wind complains all day
How some one treated him;
Nature, like us, is sometimes caught
Without her diadem.

XXX.

I THINK the hemlock likes to stand
    Upon a marge of snow;
It suits his own austerity,
And satisfies an awe

That men must slake in wilderness,
Or in the desert cloy,—
An instinct for the hoar, the bald,
Lapland's necessity.

The hemlock's nature thrives on cold;
The gnash of northern winds
Is sweetest nutriment to him,
His best Norwegian wines.

To satin races he is nought;
But children on the Don
Beneath his tabernacles play,
And Dnieper wrestlers run.

XXXI.

THERE'S a certain slant of light,
　　On winter afternoons,
That oppresses, like the weight
Of cathedral tunes.

Heavenly hurt it gives us;
We can find no scar,
But internal difference
Where the meanings are.

None may teach it anything,
'T is the seal, despair,—
An imperial affliction
Sent us of the air.

When it comes, the landscape listens,
Shadows hold their breath;
When it goes, 't is like the distance
On the look of death.

IV. TIME AND ETERNITY

I.

ONE dignity delays for all,
    One mitred afternoon.
None can avoid this purple,
None evade this crown.

Coach it insures, and footmen,
Chamber and state and throng;
Bells, also, in the village,
As we ride grand along.

What dignified attendants,
What service when we pause!
How loyally at parting
Their hundred hats they raise!

How pomp surpassing ermine,
When simple you and I
Present our meek escutcheon,
And claim the rank to die!

II.

DELAYED till she had ceased to know,
    Delayed till in its vest of snow
  Her loving bosom lay.
An hour behind the fleeting breath,
Later by just an hour than death,–
  Oh, lagging yesterday!

Could she have guessed that it would be;
Could but a crier of the glee
  Have climbed the distant hill;
Had not the bliss so slow a pace,–
Who knows but this surrendered face
  Were undefeated still?

Oh, if there may departing be
Any forgot by victory
  In her imperial round,
Show them this meek apparelled thing,
That could not stop to be a king,
  Doubtful if it be crowned!

III.

DEPARTED to the judgment,
        A mighty afternoon;
Great clouds like ushers leaning,
Creation looking on.

The flesh surrendered, cancelled,
The bodiless begun;
Two worlds, like audiences, disperse
And leave the soul alone.

IV.

SAFE in their alabaster chambers,
        Untouched by morning and untouched by noon,
Sleep the meek members of the resurrection,
Rafter of satin, and roof of stone.

Light laughs the breeze in her castle of sunshine;
Babbles the bee in a stolid ear;
Pipe the sweet birds in ignorant cadence,–
Ah, what sagacity perished here!

Grand go the years in the crescent above them;
Worlds scoop their arcs, and firmaments row,
Diadems drop and Doges surrender,
Soundless as dots on a disk of snow.

V.

ON this long storm the rainbow rose,
    On this late morn the sun;
The clouds, like listless elephants,
Horizons straggled down.

The birds rose smiling in their nests,
The gales indeed were done;
Alas! how heedless were the eyes
On whom the summer shone!

The quiet nonchalance of death
No daybreak can bestir;
The slow archangel's syllables
Must awaken her.

VI.

MY cocoon tightens, colors tease,
    I'm feeling for the air;
A dim capacity for wings
Degrades the dress I wear.

A power of butterfly must be
The aptitude to fly,
Meadows of majesty concedes
And easy sweeps of sky.

So I must baffle at the hint
And cipher at the sign,
And make much blunder, if at last
I take the clew divine.

VII.

EXULTATION is the going
        Of an inland soul to sea,—
Past the houses, past the headlands,
Into deep eternity!

Bred as we, among the mountains,
Can the sailor understand
The divine intoxication
Of the first league out from land?

VIII.

LOOK back on time with kindly eyes,
        He doubtless did his best;
How softly sinks his trembling sun
In human nature's west!

IX.

A TRAIN went through a burial gate,
      A bird broke forth and sang,
And trilled, and quivered, and shook his throat
Till all the churchyard rang;

And then adjusted his little notes,
And bowed and sang again.
Doubtless, he thought it meet of him
To say good-by to men.

X.

I DIED for beauty, but was scarce
      Adjusted in the tomb,
When one who died for truth was lain
In an adjoining room.

He questioned softly why I failed?
"For beauty," I replied.
"And I for truth,—the two are one;
We brethren are," he said.

And so, as kinsmen met a night,
We talked between the rooms,
Until the moss had reached our lips,
And covered up our names.

XI.

HOW many times these low feet staggered,
        Only the soldered mouth can tell;
Try! can you stir the awful rivet?
Try! can you lift the hasps of steel?

Stroke the cool forehead, hot so often,
Lift, if you can, the listless hair;
Handle the adamantine fingers
Never a thimble more shall wear.

Buzz the dull flies on the chamber window;
Brave shines the sun through the freckled pane;
Fearless the cobweb swings from the ceiling—
Indolent housewife, in daisies lain!

XII.

I LIKE a look of agony,
        Because I know it's true;
Men do not sham convulsion,
Nor stimulate a throe.

The eyes glaze once, and that is death.
Impossible to feign
The beads upon the forehead
By homely anguish strung.

XIII.

THAT short, potential stir
    That each can make but once,
That bustle so illustrious
'T is almost consequence,

Is the *éclat* of death.
Oh, thou unknown renown
That not a beggar would accept,
Had he the power to spurn!

XIV.

I WENT to thank her,
    But she slept;
Her bed a funnelled stone,
With nosegays at the head and foot,
That travellers had thrown,

Who went to thank her;
But she slept.
'T was short to cross the sea
To look upon her like, alive,
But turning back 't was slow.

XV.

I'VE seen a dying eye
        Run round and round a room
In search of something, as it seemed,
Then cloudier become;
And then, obscure with fog,
And then be soldered down,
Without disclosing what it be,
'T were blessed to have seen.

XVI.

THE clouds their backs together laid,
        The north begun to push,
The forests galloped till they fell,
The lightning skipped like mice;
The thunder crumbled like a stuff—
How good to be safe in tombs,
Where nature's temper cannot reach,
Nor vengeance ever comes!

XVII.

I NEVER saw a moor,
    I never saw the sea;
Yet know I how the heather looks,
And what a wave must be.

I never spoke with God,
Nor visited in heaven;
Yet certain am I of the spot
As if the chart were given.

XVIII.

GOD permits industrious angels
    Afternoons to play.
I met one,—forgot my school-mates,
All, for him, straightway.

God calls home the angels promptly
At the setting sun;
I missed mine. How dreary marbles,
After playing Crown!

XIX.

TO know just how he suffered would be dear;
      To know if any human eyes were near
To whom he could intrust his wavering gaze,
Until it settled firm on Paradise.

To know if he was patient, part content,
Was dying as he thought, or different;
Was it a pleasant day to die,
And did the sunshine face his way?

What was his furthest mind, of home, or God,
Or what the distant say
At news that he ceased human nature
On such a day?

And wishes, had he any?
Just his sigh, accented,
Had been legible to me.
And was he confident until
Ill fluttered out in everlasting well?

And if he spoke, what name was best,
What first,
What one broke off with
At the drowsiest?

Was he afraid, or tranquil?
Might he know
How conscious consciousness could grow,
Till love that was, and love too blest to be,
Meet – and the junction be Eternity?

XX.

THE last night that she lived,
          It was a common night,
Except the dying; this to us
Made nature different.

We noticed smallest things,—
Things overlooked before,
By this great light upon our minds
Italicized, as 't were.

That others could exist
While she must finish quite,
A jealousy for her arose
So nearly infinite.

We waited while she passed;
It was a narrow time,
Too jostled were our souls to speak,
At length the notice came.

She mentioned, and forgot;
Then lightly as a reed
Bent to the water, shivered scarce,
Consented, and was dead.

And we, we placed the hair,
And drew the head erect;
And then an awful leisure was,
Our faith to regulate.

XXI.

NOT in this world to see his face
            Sounds long, until I read the place
Where this is said to be
But just the primer to a life
Unopened, rare, upon the shelf,
Clasped yet to him and me.

And yet, my primer suits me so
I would not choose a book to know
Than that, be sweeter wise;
Might some one else so learned be
And leave me just my A B C,
Himself could have the skies.

XXII.

THE bustle in a house
            The morning after death
Is solemnest of industries
Enacted upon earth,—

The sweeping up the heart,
And putting love away
We shall not want to use again
Until eternity.

XXIII.

I REASON, earth is short,
         And anguish absolute.
And many hurt;
But what of that?

I reason, we could die:
The best vitality
Cannot excel decay;
But what of that?

I reason that in heaven
Somehow, it will be even,
Some new equation given;
But what of that?

XXIV.

AFRAID? Of whom am I afraid?
         Not death; for who is he?
The porter of my father's lodge
As much abasheth me.

Of life? 'T were odd I fear a thing
That comprehendeth me
In one or more existences
At Deity's decree.

Of resurrection? Is the east
Afraid to trust the morn
With her fastidious forehead?
As soon impeach my crown!

XXV.

THE sun kept setting, setting still;
        No hue of afternoon
Upon the village I perceived,–
From house to house 't was noon.

The dusk kept dropping, dropping still;
No dew upon the grass,
But only on my forehead stopped,
And wandered in my face.

My feet kept drowsing, drowsing still,
My fingers were awake;
Yet why so little sound myself
Unto my seeming make?

How well I knew the light before!
I could not see it now.
'T is dying, I am doing; but
I'm not afraid to know.

XXVI.

TWO swimmers wrestled on the spar
        Until the morning sun,
When one turned smiling to the land.
O God, the other one!

The stray ships passing spied a face
Upon the waters borne,
With eyes in death still begging raised,
And hands beseeching thrown.

XXVII.

BECAUSE I could not stop for Death,
    He kindly stopped for me;
The carriage held but just ourselves
And Immortality.

We slowly drove, he knew no haste,
And I had put away
My labor, and my leisure too,
For his civility.

We passed the school where children played,
Their lessons scarcely done;
We passed the fields of gazing grain,
We passed the setting sun.

We paused before a house that seemed
A swelling of the ground;
The roof was scarcely visible,
The cornice but a mound.

Since then 't is centuries; but each
Feels shorter than the day
I first surmised the horses' heads
Were toward eternity.

XXVIII.

SHE went as quiet as the dew
        From a familiar flower.
Not like the dew did she return
At the accustomed hour!

She dropt as softly as a star
From out my summer's eve;
Less skilful than Leverrier
It's sorer to believe!

XXIX.

AT last to be identified!
        At last, the lamps upon thy side,
The rest of life to see!
Past midnight, past the morning star!
Past sunrise! Ah! what leagues there are
Between our feet and day!

XXX.

EXCEPT to heaven, she is nought;
        Except for angels, lone;
Except to some wide-wandering bee,
A flower superfluous blown;

Except for winds, provincial;
Except by butterflies,
Unnoticed as a single dew
That on the acre lies.

The smallest housewife in the grass,
Yet take her from the lawn,
And somebody has lost the face
That made existence home!

XXXI.

DEATH is a dialogue between
        The spirit and the dust.
"Dissolve," says Death. The Spirit, "Sir,
I have another trust."

Death doubts it, argues from the ground.
The Spirit turns away,
Just laying off, for evidence,
An overcoat of clay.

XXXII.

IT was too late for man,
          But early yet for God;
Creation impotent to help,
But prayer remained our side.

How excellent the heaven,
When earth cannot be had;
How hospitable, then, the face
Of our old neighbor, God!

XXXIII.

WHEN I was small, a woman
          died.
          To-day her only boy
Went up from the Potomac,
His face all victory,

To look at her; how slowly
The seasons must have turned
Till bullets clipt an angle,
And he passed quickly round!

If pride shall be in Paradise
I never can decide;
Of their imperial conduct,
No person testified.

But proud in apparition,
That woman and her boy
Pass back and forth before my brain,
As ever in the sky.

XXXIV.

THE daisy follows soft the sun,
  And when his golden walk is done,
 Sits shyly at his feet.
He, waking, finds the flower near.
"Wherefore, marauder, art thou here?
 "Because, sir, love is sweet!"

We are the flower, Thou the sun!
Forgive us, if as days decline,
 We nearer steal to Thee,—
Enamoured of the parting west,
The peace, the flight, the amethyst,
 Night's possibility!

XXXV.

NO rack can torture me,
    My soul's at liberty.
Behind this mortal bone
There knits a bolder one

You cannot prick with saw,
Nor rend with scymitar.
Two bodies therefore be;
Bind one, and one will flee.

The eagle of his nest
No easier divest
And gain the sky,
Than mayest thou,

Except thyself may be
Thine enemy;
Captivity is consciousness,
So's liberty.

XXXVI.

I LOST a world the other day.
        Has anybody found?
You'll know it by the row of stars
Around its forehead bound.

A rich man might not notice it;
Yet to my frugal eye
Of more esteem than ducats.
Oh, find it, sir, for me!

XXXVII.

IF I should n't be alive
        When the robins come,
Give the one in red cravat
A memorial crumb.

If I could n't thank you,
Being just asleep,
You will know I'm trying
With my granite lip!

XXXVIII.

SLEEP is supposed to be,
        By souls of sanity,
The shutting of the eye.

Sleep is the station grand
Down which on either hand
The hosts of witness stand!

Morn is supposed to be,
By people of degree,
The breaking of the day.

Morning has not occurred!
That shall aurora be
East of eternity;

One with the banner gay,
One in the red array,–
That is the break of day.

XXXIX.

I SHALL know why, when time is over,
    And I have ceased to wonder why;
Christ will explain each separate anguish
In the fair schoolroom of the sky.

He will tell me what Peter promised,
And I, for wonder at his woe,
I shall forget the drop of anguish
That scalds me now, that scalds me now.

XL.

I NEVER lost as much but twice,
    And that was in the sod;
Twice have I stood a beggar
Before the door of God!

Angels, twice descending,
Reimbursed my store.
Burglar, banker, father,
I am poor once more!

. . .

POEMS

BY

EMILY DICKINSON

· SECOND SERIES ·

. . .

PREFACE

THE eagerness with which the first volume of Emily
Dickinson's poems has been read shows very clearly
that all our alleged modern artificiality does not prevent a
prompt appreciation of the qualities of directness and
simplicity in approaching the greatest themes,—life and love
and death. That "irresistible needle-touch," as one of her best
critics has called it, piercing at once the very core of a thought,
has found a response as wide and sympathetic as it has been
unexpected even to those who knew best her compelling power.
This second volume, while open to the same criticism as to
form with its predecessor, shows also the same shining beauties.

Although Emily Dickinson had been in the habit of sending
occasional poems to friends and correspondents, the full extent
of her writing was by no means imagined by them. Her friend
"H.H." must at least have suspected it, for in a letter dated 5th
September, 1884, she wrote:—

MY DEAR FRIEND,—What portfolios full of verses you must
have! It is a cruel wrong to your "day and generation" that you
will not give them light.

If such a thing should happen as that I should outlive you, I
wish you would make me your literary legatee and executor.
Surely after you are what is called "dead" you will be willing
that the poor ghosts you have left behind should be cheered
and pleased by your verses, will you not? You ought to be. I do
not think we have a right to withhold from the world a word or
a thought any more than a *deed* which might help a single
soul. . . .

Truly yours,

HELEN JACKSON.

The "portfolios" were found, shortly after Emily Dickinson's death, by her sister and only surviving housemate. Most of the poems had been carefully copied on sheets of note-paper, and tied in little fascicules, each of six or eight sheets. While many of them bear evidence of having been thrown off at white heat, still more had received thoughtful revision. There is the frequent addition of rather perplexing foot-notes, affording large choice of words and phrases. And in the copies which she sent to friends, sometimes one form, sometimes another, is found to have been used. Without important exception, her friends have generously placed at the disposal of the Editors any poems they had received from her; and these have given the obvious advantage of comparison among several renderings of the same verse.

To what further rigorous pruning her verses would have been subjected had she published them herself, we cannot know. They should be regarded in many cases as merely the first strong and suggestive sketches of an artist, intended to be embodied at some time in the finished picture.

Emily Dickinson appears to have written her first poems in the winter of 1862. In a letter to one of the present Editors the April following, she says, "I made no verse, but one or two, until this winter."

The handwriting was at first somewhat like the delicate, running Italian hand of our elder gentlewomen; but as she advanced in breadth of thought, it grew bolder and more abrupt, until in her latest years each letter stood distinct and separate from its fellows. In most of her poems, particularly the later ones, everything by way of punctuation was discarded, except numerous dashes; and all important words began with capitals. The effect of a page of her more recent manuscript is exceedingly quaint and strong. Although there is nowhere a date, the handwriting makes it possible to arrange the poems with general chronologic accuracy. . . .

The variation of readings, with the fact that she often wrote in pencil and not always clearly, have at times thrown a good deal of responsibility upon her Editors. But all interference not absolutely inevitable has been avoided. The very roughness of her own rendering is part of herself, and not lightly to be touched; for it seems in many cases that she intentionally avoided the smoother and more usual rhymes.

Like impressionist pictures or Wagner's rugged music, the very absence of conventional form challenges attention. In Emily Dickinson's exacting hands the especial, intrinsic fitness of a particular order of words might not be sacrificed to anything virtually extrinsic; and her verses all show a strange cadence of inner rhythmical music. Lines are always daringly constructed, and the "thought-rhyme" appears frequently,– appealing, indeed, to an unrecognized sense more elusive than hearing.

Emily Dickinson scrutinized everything with clear-eyed frankness. Every subject was proper ground for legitimate study, even the sombre facts of death and burial, and the unknown life beyond. She touches these themes sometimes lightly, sometimes almost humorously, more often with weird and peculiar power; but she is never by any chance frivolous or trivial. And while, as one critic has said, she may exhibit toward God "an Emersonian self-possession," it was because she looked upon all life with a candor as unprejudiced as it is rare.

She had tried society and the world, and found them lacking. She was not an invalid, and she lived in seclusion from no love-disappointment. Her life was the normal blossoming of a nature introspective to a high degree, whose best thought could not exist in pretence.

Storm, wind, the wild March sky, sunsets and dawns; the birds and bees, butterflies and flowers of her garden, with a few trusted human friends, were sufficient companionship. The coming of the first robin was a jubilee beyond drowning of monarch or birthday of pope; the first red leaf hurrying through "the altered air," an epoch. Immortality was close about her; and while never morbid or melancholy, she lived in its presence.

MABEL LOOMIS TODD.

AMHERST, MASSACHUSETTS,
August 1891.

. . .

PRELUDE

My nosegays are for captives;
Dim, long-expectant eyes,
Fingers denied the plucking,
Patient till paradise.

To such, if they should whisper
Of morning and the moor,
They bear no other errand,
And I, no other prayer.

I. LIFE

I.

I'M nobody! Who are you?
　　Are you nobody, too?
Then there's a pair of us–don't tell!
They'd banish us, you know.

How dreary to be somebody!
How public, like a frog
To tell your name the livelong day
To an admiring bog!

II.

I BRING an unaccustomed wine
　　To lips long parching, next to mine,
And summon them to drink.

Crackling with fever, they essay;
I turn my brimming eyes away,
And come next hour to look.

The hands still hug the tardy glass;
The lips I would have cooled, alas!
Are so superfluous cold,

I would as soon attempt to warm
The bosoms where the frost has lain
Ages beneath the mould.

Some other thirsty there may be
To whom this would have pointed me
Had it remained to speak.

And so I always bear the cup
If haply, mine may be the drop
Some pilgrim thirst to slake,–

If, haply, any say to me,
"Unto the little, unto me,"
When I at last awake.

III.

THE nearest dream recedes, unrealized.
  The heaven we chase
  Like the June bee
  Before the school-boy
  Invites the race;
  Stoops to an easy clover–
Dips–evades–teases–deploys;
  Then to the royal clouds
  Lifts his light pinnace
  Heedless of the boy
Staring, bewildered, at the mocking sky.

  Homesick for steadfast honey,
  Ah! the bee flies not
That brews that rare variety.

IV.

WE play at paste,
        Till qualified for pearl,
Then drop the paste,
And deem ourself a fool.
The shapes, though, were similar,
And our new hands
Learned gem-tactics
Practising sands.

V.

I FOUND the phrase to every thought
        I ever had, but one;
And that defies me,—as a hand
Did try to chalk the sun

To races nurtured in the dark;—
How would your own begin?
Can blaze be done in cochineal,
Or noon in mazarin?

VI.

HOPE is the thing with feathers
          That perches in the soul,
And sings the tune without the words,
And never stops at all,

And sweetest in the gale is heard;
And sore must be the storm
That could abash the little bird
That kept so many warm.

I've heard it in the chillest land,
And on the strangest sea;
Yet, never, in extremity,
It asked a crumb of me.

VII.

DARE you see a soul at the white heat?
          Then crouch within the door.
Red is the fire's common tint;
     But when the vivid ore

Has sated flame's conditions,
     Its quivering substance plays
Without a color but the light
     Of unanointed blaze.

Least village boasts its blacksmith,
     Whose anvil's even din
Stands symbol for the finer forge
That soundless tugs within,

Refining these impatient ores
   With hammer and with blaze,
Until the designated light
   Repudiate the forge.

VIII.

WHO never lost, are unprepared
   A coronet to find;
Who never thirsted, flagons
And cooling tamarind.

Who never climbed the weary league —
Can such a foot explore
The purple territories
On Pizarro's shore?

How many legions overcome?
The emperor will say.
How many colors taken
On Revolution Day?

How many bullets bearest?
The royal scar hast thou?
Angels, write "Promoted"
On this soldier's brow!

IX.

I CAN wade grief,
          Whole pools of it,–
I'm used to that.
But the least push of joy
Breaks up my feet,
And I tip–drunken.
Let no pebble smile,
'T was the new liquor,–
That was all!

Power is only pain,
Stranded, through discipline,
Till weights will hang.
Give balm to giants,
And they'll wilt, like men.
Give Himmaleh,–
They'll carry him!

X.

I NEVER hear the word "escape"
          Without a quicker blood,
A sudden expectation,
A flying attitude.

I never hear of prisons broad
By soldiers battered down,
But I tug childish at my bars,–
Only to fail again!

XI.

FOR each ecstatic instant
        We must an anguish pay
In keen and quivering ratio
To the ecstasy.

For each beloved hour
Sharp pittances of years,
Bitter contested farthings
And coffers heaped with tears.

XII.

THROUGH the straight pass of suffering
        The martyrs even trod,
Their feet upon temptation,
Their faces upon God.

A stately, shriven company;
Convulsion playing round,
Harmless as streaks of meteor
Upon a planet's bound.

Their faith the everlasting troth;
Their expectation fair;
The needle to the north degree
Wades so, through polar air.

XIII.

I MEANT to have but modest needs,
        Such as content, and heaven;
Within my income these could lie,
And life and I keep even.

But since the last included both,
It would suffice my prayer
But just for one to stipulate,
And grace would grant the pair.

And so, upon this wise I prayed,–
Great Spirit, give to me
A heaven not so large as yours,
But large enough for me.

A smile suffused Jehovah's face;
The cherubim withdrew;
Grave saints stole out to look at me,
And showed their dimples, too.

I left the place with all my might,–
My prayer away I threw;
The quiet ages picked it up,
And Judgment twinkled, too,

That one so honest be extant
As take the tale for true
That "Whatsoever you shall ask,
Itself be given you."

But I, grown shrewder, scan the skies
With a suspicious air,–
As children, swindled for the first,
All swindlers be, infer.

XIV.

THE thought beneath so slight a film
    Is more distinctly seen,–
As laces just reveal the surge,
Or mists the Apennine.

XV.

THE soul unto itself
    Is an imperial friend,–
Or the most agonizing spy
An enemy could send.

Secure against its own,
No treason it can fear;
Itself its sovereign, of itself
The soul should stand in awe.

XVI.

SURGEONS must be very careful
        When they take the knife!
Underneath their fine incisions
Stirs the culprit,—Life!

XVII.

I LIKE to see it lap the miles,
        And lick the valleys up,
And stop to feed itself at tanks;
Ant then, prodigious, step

Around a pile of mountains,
And, supercilious, peer
In shanties by the sides of roads;
And then a quarry pare

To fit its sides, and crawl between,
Complaining all the while
In horrid, hooting stanza;
Then chase itself down hill

And neigh like Boanerges;
Then, punctual as a star,
Stop—docile and omnipotent—
At its own stable door.

XVIII.

THE show is not the show,
        But they that go.
Menagerie to me
My neighbor be.
Fair play—
Both went to see.

XIX.

DELIGHT becomes pictorial
        When viewed through pain,—
More fair, because impossible
That any gain.

The mountain at a given distance
In amber lies;
Approached, the amber flits a little,—
And that's the skies!

XX.

A THOUGHT went up my mind to-day
        That I have had before,
But did not finish,—some way back,
I could not fix the year,

Nor where it went, nor why it came
The second time to me,
Nor definitely what it was,
Have I the art to say.

But somewhere in my soul, I know
I've met the thing before;
It just reminded me—'t was all—
And came my way no more.

XXI.

IS Heaven a physician?
        They say that He can heal;
But medicine posthumous
    Is unavailable.

Is Heaven an exchequer?
    They speak of what we owe;
But that negotiation
    I'm not a party to.

XXII.

THOUGH I get home how late, how late!
    So I get home, 't will compensate.
Better will be the ecstasy
That they have done expecting me,
When, night descending, dumb and dark,
They hear my unexpected knock.
Transporting must the moment be
Brewed from decades of agony!

To think just how the fire will burn,
Just how long-cheated eyes will turn
To wonder what myself will say,
And what itself will say to me,
Beguiles the centuries of way!

XXIII.

A POOR torn heart, a tattered heart,
    That sat it down to rest,
Nor noticed that the ebbing day
Flowed silver to the west,
Nor noticed night did soft descend
Nor constellation burn,
Intent upon the vision
Of latitudes unknown.

The angels, happening that way,
This dusty heart espied;
Tenderly took it up from toil
And carried it to God.
There,—sandals for the barefoot;
There,—gathered from the gales,
Do the blue havens by the hand
Lead the wandering sails.

XXIV.

I SHOULD have been too glad, I see,
        Too lifted for the scant degree
    Of life's penurious round;
My little circuit would have shamed
This new circumference, have blamed
    The homelier time behind.

I should have been too saved, I see,
Too rescued; fear too dim to me
    That I could spell the prayer
I knew so perfect yesterday,—
That scalding one, "Sabachthani,"
    Recited fluent here.

Earth would have been too much, I see,
And heaven not enough for me;
    I should have had the joy
Without the fear to justify,—
The palm without the Calvary;
    So, Saviour, crucify.

Defeat whets victory, they say;
The reefs in old Gethsemane
    Endear the shore beyond.
'T is beggars banquets best define;
'T is thirsting vitalizes wine,—
    Faith faints to understand.

XXV.

IT tossed and tossed,–
        A little brig I knew,–
O'ertook by blast,
It spun and spun,
And groped delirious, for morn.

It slipped and slipped,
As one that drunken stepped;
Its white foot tripped,
Then dropped from sight.

Ah, brig, good-night
To crew and you;
The ocean's heart too smooth, too blue,
To break for you.

XXVI.

VICTORY comes late,
        And is held low to freezing lips
Too rapt with frost
To take it.
How sweet it would have tasted,
Just a drop!
Was God so economical?
His table's spread too high for us
Unless we dine on tip-toe.
Crumbs fit such little mouths,
Cherries suit robins;
The eagle's golden breakfast
Strangles them.
God keeps his oath to sparrows,
Who of little love
Know how to starve!

XXXVII.

GOD gave a loaf to every bird,
        But just a crumb to me;
I dare not eat it, though I starve,—
My poignant luxury
To own it, touch it, prove the feat
That made the pellet mine,—
Too happy in my sparrow chance
For ampler coveting.

It might be famine all around,
I could not miss an ear,
Such plenty smiles upon my board,
My garner shows so fair.
I wonder how the rich may feel,—
An Indiaman—an Earl?
I deem that I with but a crumb
Am sovereign of them all.

XXVIII.

EXPERIMENT to me
        Is every one I meet
If it contain a kernel?
The figure of a nut

Presents upon a tree,
Equally plausibly;
But meat within is requisite,
To squirrels and to me.

XXIX.

MY country need not change her gown,
    Her triple suit as sweet
As when 't was cut at Lexington,
And first pronounced "a fit."

Great Britain disapproves "the stars;"
Disparagement discreet,—
There's something in their attitude
That taunts her bayonet.

XXX.

FAITH is a fine invention
    For gentlemen who see;
But microscopes are prudent
In an emergency!

XXXI.

EXCEPT the heaven had come so near,
        So seemed to choose my door,
The distance would not haunt me so;
I had not hoped before.

But just to hear the grace depart
I never thought to see,
Afflicts me with a double loss;
'T is lost, and lost to me.

XXXII.

PORTRAITS are to daily faces
        As an evening west
To a fine, pedantic sunshine
In a satin vest.

XXXIII.

I TOOK my power in my hand
        And went against the world;
'T was not so much as David had,
But I was twice as bold.

I aimed my pebble, but myself
Was all the one that fell.
Was it Goliath was too large,
Or only I too small?

XXXIV.

A SHADY friend for torrid days
        Is easier to find
Than one of higher temperature
For frigid hour of mind.

The vane a little to the east
Scares muslin souls away;
If broadcloth breasts are firmer
Than those of organdy,

Who is to blame? The weaver?
Ah! the bewildering thread!
The tapestries of paradise
So notelessly are made!

XXXV.

EACH life converges to some centre
          Expressed or still;
Exists in every human nature
A goal,

Admitted scarcely to itself, it may be,
Too fair
For credibility's temerity
To dare.

Adored with caution, as a brittle heaven,
To reach
Were hopeless as the rainbow's raiment
To touch,

Yet persevered toward, surer for the distance;
How high
Unto the saints' slow diligence
The sky!

Ungained, it may be, by a life's low venture,
But then,
Eternity enables the endeavoring
Again.

XXXVI.

BEFORE I got my eye put out,
    I liked as well to see
As other creatures that have eyes,
And know no other way.

But were it told to me, to-day,
That I might have the sky
For mine, I tell you that my heart
Would split, for size of me.

The meadows mine, the mountains mine, –
All forests, stintless stars,
As much of noon as I could take
Between my finite eyes.

The motions of the dipping birds,
The lightning's jointed road,
For mine to look at when I liked, –
The news would strike me dead!

So, safer, guess, with just my soul
Upon the window-pane
Where other creatures put their eyes,
Incautious of the sun.

XXXVII.

TALK with prudence to a beggar
     Of 'Potosi' and the mines!
Reverently to the hungry
Of your viands and your wines!

Cautious, hint to any captive
You have passed enfranchised feet!
Anecdotes of air in dungeons
Have sometimes proved deadly sweet!

XXXVIII.

HE preached upon "breadth" till it argued
     him narrow,–
The broad are too broad to define;
And of "truth" until it proclaimed him a liar,–
The truth never flaunted a sign.

Simplicity fled from his counterfeit presence
As gold the pyrites would shun.
What confusion would cover the innocent Jesus
To meet so enabled a man!

XXXIX.

GOOD night! which put the candle out?
　　　A jealous zephyr, not a doubt.
Ah! friend, you little knew
How long at that celestial wick
The angels labored diligent;
　　　Extinguished, now, for you!

It might have been the lighthouse spark
Some sailor, rowing in the dark,
　　　Had importuned to see!
It might have been the waning lamp
That lit the drummer from the camp
　　　To purer reveille!

XL.

WHEN I hoped I feared,
　　　Since I hoped I dared;
Everywhere alone
As a church remain;
Spectre cannot harm,
Serpent cannot charm;
He deposes doom,
Who hath suffered him.

XLI.

A DEED knocks first at thought,
          And then it knocks at will.
That is the manufacturing spot,
And will at home and well.

It then goes out an act,
Or is entombed so still
That only to the ear of God
Its doom is audible.

XLII.

MINE enemy is growing old,–
          I have at last revenge.
The palate of the hate departs;
If any would avenge,–

Let him be quick, the viand flits,
It is a faded meat.
Anger as soon as fed is dead;
'T is starving makes it fat.

XLIII.

REMORSE is memory awake,
      Her companies astir,—
A presence of departed acts
At window and at door.

It's past set down before the soul,
And lighted with a match,
Perusal to facilitate
Of its condensed despatch.

Remorse is cureless,—the disease
Not even God can heal;
For 't is his institution,—
The complement of hell.

XLIV.

THE body grows outside,—
      The more convenient way,—
That if the spirit like to hide,
Its temple stands alway

Ajar, secure, inviting;
It never did betray
The soul that asked its shelter
In timid honesty.

XLV.

UNDUE significance a starving man attaches
        To food
Far off; he sighs, and therefore hopeless,
And therefore good.

Partaken, it relieves indeed, but proves us
That spices fly
In the receipt. It was the distance
Was savory.

XLVI.

HEART not so heavy as mine,
        Wending late home,
As it passed my window
Whistled itself a tune,–

A careless snatch, a ballad,
A ditty of the street;
Yet to my irritated ear
An anodyne so sweet,

It was as if a bobolink,
Sauntering this way,
Carolled and mused and carolled,
Then bubbled slow away.

It was as if a chirping brook
Upon a toilsome way
Set bleeding feet to minuets
Without the knowing why.

To-morrow, night will come again,
Weary, perhaps, and sore.
Ah, bugle, by my window,
I pray you stroll once more!

XLVII.

I MANY times thought peace had come,
    When peace was far away;
As wrecked men deem they sight the land
At centre of the sea,

And struggle slacker, but to prove,
As hopelessly as I,
How many the fictitious shores
Before the harbor lie.

XLVIII.

UNTO my books so good to turn
        Far ends of tired days;
It half endears the abstinence,
And pain is missed in praise.

As flavors cheer retarded guests
With banquetings to be,
So spices stimulate the time
Till my small library.

It may be wilderness without,
Far feet of failing men,
But holiday excludes the night,
And it is bells within.

I thank these kinsmen of the shelf;
Their countenances bland
Enamour in prospective,
And satisfy, obtained.

XLIX.

THIS merit hath the worst,--
        It cannot be again.
When Fate hath taunted last
And thrown her furthest stone,

The maimed may pause and breathe,
And glance securely round.
The deer invites no longer
Than it eludes the hound.

L.

I HAD been hungry all the years;
      My noon had come, to dine;
I trembling, drew the table near,
And touched the curious wine.

'T was this on tables I had seen,
When turning, hungry, lone,
I looked in windows, for the wealth
I could not hope to own.

I did not know the ample bread,
'T was so unlike the crumb
The birds and I had often shared
In Nature's dining-room

The plenty hurt me, 't was so new,—
Myself felt ill and odd,
As berry of a mountain bush
Transplanted to the road.

Nor was I hungry; so I found
That hunger was a way
Of persons outside windows,
The entering takes away.

LI.

I GAINED it so,
       By climbing slow,
By catching at the twigs that grow
Between the bliss and me.
       It hung so high,
       As well the sky
       Attempt by strategy.

I said I gained it,–
       This was all.
Look, how I clutch it,
       Lest it fall,
And I a pauper go;
Unfitted by an instant's grace
For the contented beggar's face
I wore an hour ago.

LII.

TO learn the transport by the pain,
　　As blind men learn the sun;
To die of thirst, suspecting
That brooks in meadows run;

To stay the homesick, homesick feet
Upon a foreign shore
Haunted by native lands, the while,
And blue, beloved air—

This is the sovereign anguish,
This, the signal woe!
These are the patient laureates
Whose voices, trained below,

Ascend in ceaseless carol,
Inaudible, indeed,
To us, the duller scholars
Of the mysterious bard!

LIII.

I YEARS had been from home,
    And now, before the door,
I dared not open, lest a face
I never saw before

Stare vacant into mine
And ask my business there.
My business,—just a life I left,
Was such still dwelling there?

I fumbled at my nerve,
I scanned the windows near;
The silence like an ocean rolled,
And broke against my ear.

I laughed a wooden laugh
That I could fear a door,
Who danger and the dead had faced,
But never quaked before.

I fitted to the latch
My hand, with trembling care,
Lest back the awful door should spring,
And leave me standing there.

I moved my fingers off
As cautiously as glass,
And held my ears, and like a thief
Fled gasping from the house.

LIV.

PRAYER is the little implement
          Through which men reach
Where presence is denied them.
They fling their speech

By means of it in God's ear;
If then He hear,
This sums the apparatus
Comprised in prayer.

LV.

I KNOW that he exists
          Somewhere, in silence.
He has hid his rare life
From our gross eyes.

'T is an instant's play,
'T is a fond ambush,
Just to make bliss
Earn her own surprise!

But should the play
Prove piercing earnest,
Should the glee glaze
In death's stiff stare,

Would not the fun
Look too expensive?
Would not the jest
Have crawled too far?

LVI.

MUSICIANS wrestle everywhere:
    All day, among the crowded air,
  I hear the silver strife;
And – waking long before the dawn –
Such transport breaks upon the town
  I think it that "new life!"

It is not bird, it has no nest;
Nor band, in brass and scarlet dressed,
  Nor tambourine, nor man;
It is not hymn from pulpit read,–
The morning stars the treble led
  On time's first afternoon!

Some say it is the spheres at play!
Some say that bright majority
  Of vanished dames and men!
Some think it service in the place
Where we, with late, celestial face,
  Please God, shall ascertain!

LVII.

JUST lost when I was saved!
        Just felt the world go by!
Just girt me for the onset with eternity,
When breath blew back,
And on the other side
I heard recede the disappointed tide!

Therefore, as one returned, I feel,
Odd secrets of the line to tell!
Some sailor, skirting foreign shores,
Some pale reporter from the awful doors
Before the seal!

Next time, to Stay!
Next time, the things to see
By ear unheard,
Unscrutinized by eye.

Next time, to tarry,
While the ages steal,–
Slow tramp the centuries,
And the cycles wheel.

II. LOVE

I.

OF all the souls that stand create
     I have elected one.
When sense from spirit files away,
And subterfuge is done;

When that which is and that which was
Apart, intrinsic, stand,
And this brief tragedy of flesh
Is shifted like a sand;

When figures show their royal front
And mists are carved away,–
Behold the atom I preferred
To all the lists of clay!

II.

I HAVE no life but this,
     To lead it here;
Nor any death, but lest
Dispelled from there;

Nor tie to earths to come,
Nor action new,
Except through this extent,
The realm of you.

III.

YOUR riches taught me poverty.
　　Myself a millionnaire
In little wealths—as girls could boast,—
Till broad as Buenos Ayre,

You drifted your dominions
A different Peru;
And I esteemed all poverty,
For life's estate with you.

Of mines I little know, myself,
But just the names of gems,—
The colors of the commonest;
And scarce of diadems

So much that, did I meet the queen,
Her glory I should know:
But this must be a different wealth,
To miss it beggars so.

I'm sure 't is India all day
To those who look on you
Without a stint, without a blame,–
Might I but be the Jew!

I'm sure it is Golconda,
Beyond my power to deem,–
To have a smile for mine each day,
How better than a gem!

At least, it solaces to know
That there exists a gold,
Although I prove it just in time
Its distance to behold!

It's far, far treasure to surmise,
And estimate the pearl
That slipped my simple fingers through
While just a girl at school!

IV.

I GAVE myself to him,
　　　And took himself for pay.
The solemn contract of a life
Was ratified this way.

The wealth might disappoint,
Myself a poorer prove
Than this great purchaser suspect,
The daily own of Love

Depreciate the vision;
But, till the merchant buy,
Still fable, in the isles of spice,
The subtle cargoes lie.

At least, 't is mutual risk,—
Some found it mutual gain;
Sweet debt of Life—each night to owe,
Insolvent, every noon.

V.

"GOING to him! Happy letter! Tell him —
          Tell him the page I did n't write;
Tell him I only said the syntax,
And left the verb and the pronoun out.
Tell him just how the fingers hurried,
Then how they waded, slow, slow, slow;
And then you wished you had eyes in your pages,
So you could see what moved them so.

"Tell him it was n't a practised writer,
You guessed, from the way the sentence toiled;
You could hear the bodice tug, behind you,
As if it held but the might of a child;
You almost pitied it, you, it worked so.
Tell him — No, you may quibble there,
For it would split his heart to know it,
And then you and I were silenter.

"Tell him night finished before we finished,
And the old clock kept neighing 'day!'
And you got sleepy and begged to be ended —
What could it hinder so, to say?
Tell him just how she sealed you, cautious,
But if he ask where you are hid
Until to-morrow, — happy letter!
Gesture, coquette, and shake your head!"

VI.

THE way I read a letter's this:
　　'T is first I lock the door,
And push it with my fingers next,
For transport it be sure.

And then I go the furthest off
To counteract a knock;
Then draw my little letter forth
And softly pick its lock.

Then, glancing narrow at the wall,
And narrow at the floor,
For firm conviction of a mouse
Not exorcised before,

Peruse how infinite I am
To—no one that you know!
And sigh for lack of heaven,—but not
The heaven the creeds bestow.

VII.

WILD nights! Wild nights!
        Were I with thee,
Wild nights should be
Our luxury!

Futile the winds
To a heart in port,–
Done with the compass,
Done with the chart.

Rowing in Eden!
Ah! the sea!
Might I but moor
To-night in thee!

VIII.

THE night was wide, and furnished scant
    With but a single star,
That often as a cloud it met
Blew out itself for fear.

The wind pursued the little bush,
And drove away the leaves
November left; then clambered up
And fretted in the eaves.

No squirrel went abroad;
A dog's belated feet
Like intermittent plush were heard
Adown the empty street.

To feel if blinds be fast,
And closer to the fire
Her little rocking-chair to draw,
And shiver for the poor,

The housewife's gentle task.
"How pleasanter," said she
Unto the sofa opposite,
"The sleet than May—no thee!"

IX.

D^{ID} the harebell loose her girdle
　　　To the lover bee,
Would the bee the harebell hallow
Much as formerly?

Did the paradise, persuaded,
Yield her moat of pearl,
Would the Eden be an Eden,
Or the earl an earl?

X.

A CHARM invests a face
　　　Imperfectly beheld,—
The lady dare not lift her veil
For fear it be dispelled.

But peers beyond her mesh,
And wishes, and denies,—
Lest interview annul a want
That image satisfies.

XI.

THE rose did caper on her cheek,
    Her bodice rose and fell,
Her pretty speech, like drunken men,
Did stagger pitiful.

Her fingers fumbled at her work,–
Her needle would not go;
What ailed so smart a little maid
It puzzled me to know,

Till opposite I spied a cheek
That bore another rose;
Just opposite, another speech
That like the drunkard goes;

A vest that, like the bodice, danced
To the immortal tune,–
Till those two troubled little clocks
Ticked softly into one.

XII.

IN lands I never saw, they say,
        Immortal Alps look down,
Whose bonnets touch the firmament,
Whose sandals touch the town,–

Meek at whose everlasting feet
A myriad daisies play.
Which, sir, are you, and which am I,
Upon an August day?

XIII.

THE moon is distant from the sea,
        And yet with amber hands
She leads him, docile as a boy,
Along appointed sands.

He never misses a degree;
Obedient to her eye,
He comes just so far toward the town,
Just so far goes away.

Oh, Signor, thine the amber hand,
And mine the distant sea,–
Obedient to the least command
Thine eyes impose on me.

XIV.

HE put the belt around my life,—
    I heard the buckle snap,
And turned away, imperial,
My lifetime folding up
Deliberate, as a duke would do
A kingdom's title-deed,—
Henceforth a dedicated sort,
A member of the cloud.

Yet not too far to come at call,
And do the little toils
That make the circuit of the rest,
And deal occasional smiles
To lives that stoop to notice mine
And kindly ask it in,—
Whose invitation, knew you not
For whom I must decline?

XV.

I HELD a jewel in my fingers
    And went to sleep.
The day was warm, and winds were prosy;
I said: "'T will keep."

I woke and chid my honest fingers,—
The gem was gone;
And now an amethyst remembrance
Is all I own.

XVI.

WHAT if I say I shall not wait?
        What if I burst the fleshly gate
And pass, escaped, to thee?
What if I file this mortal off,
See where it hurt me,–that's enough,–
And wade in liberty?

They cannot take us any more,–
Dungeons may call, and guns implore;
Unmeaning now, to me,
As laughter was an hour ago,
Or laces, or a travelling show,
Or who died yesterday!

III. NATURE

I.

NATURE, the gentlest mother,
    Impatient of no child,
The feeblest or the waywardest,–
Her admonition mild

In forest and the hill
By traveller is heard,
Restraining rampant squirrel
Or too impetuous bird.

How fair her conversation,
A summer afternoon,–
Her household, her assembly;
And when the sun goes down

Her voice among the aisles
Incites the timid prayer
Of the minutest cricket,
The most unworthy flower.

When all the children sleep
She turns as long away
As will suffice to light her lamps;
Then, bending from the sky

With infinite affection
And infiniter care,
Her golden finger on her lip,
Wills silence everywhere.

II.

WILL there really be a morning?
      Is there such a thing as day?
Could I see it from the mountains
If I were as tall as they?

Has it feet like water-lilies?
Has it feathers like a bird?
Is it brought from famous countries
Of which I have never heard?

Oh, some scholar! Oh, some sailor!
Oh, some wise man from the skies!
Please to tell a little pilgrim
Where the place called morning lies!

III.

AT half-past three a single bird
      Unto a silent sky
Propounded but a single term
Of cautious melody.

At half-past four, experiment
Had subjugated test,
And lo! her silver principle
Supplanted all the rest.

At half-past seven, element
Nor implement was seen,
And place was where the presence was,
Circumference between.

IV.

THE day came slow, till five o'clock,
    Then sprang before the hills
Like hindered rubies, or the light
A sudden musket spills.

The purple could not keep the east,
The sunrise shook from fold,
Like breadths of topaz, packed a night,
The lady just unrolled.

The happy winds their timbrels took;
The birds, in docile rows,
Arranged themselves around their prince
(The wind is prince of those).

The orchard sparkled like a Jew,–
How mighty 't was, to stay
A guest in this stupendous place,
The parlor of the day!

V.

THE sun just touched the morning;
    The morning, happy thing,
Supposed that he had come to dwell,
And life would be all spring.

She felt herself supremer,—
    raised, ethereal thing;
Henceforth for her what holiday!
Meanwhile, her wheeling king

Trailed slow along the orchards
His haughty, spangled hems.
Leaving a new necessity,—
The want of diadems!

The morning fluttered, staggered,
Felt feebly for her crown,—
Her unanointed forehead
Henceforth her only one.

VI.

THE robin is the one
    That interrupts the morn
With hurried, few, express reports
When March is scarcely on.

The robin is the one
That overflows the noon
With her cherubic quantity,
An April but begun.

The robin is the one
That speechless from her nest
Submits that home and certainty
And sanctity are best.

VII.

FROM cocoon forth a butterfly
        As lady from her door
Emerged—a summer afternoon—
Repairing everywhere,

Without design, that I could trace,
Except to stray abroad
On miscellaneous enterprise
The clovers understood.

Her pretty parasol was seen
Contracting in a field
Where men made hay, then struggling hard
With an opposing cloud,

Where parties, phantom as herself,
To Nowhere seemed to go
In purposeless circumference,
As 't were a tropic show.

And notwithstanding bee that worked,
And flower that zealous blew,
This audience of idleness
Disdained them, from the sky,

Till sundown crept, a steady tide,
And men that made the hay,
And afternoon, and butterfly,
Extinguished in its sea.

VIII.

BEFORE you thought of spring,
        Except as a surmise,
You see, God bless his sud-
denness,
A fellow in the skies
Of independent hues,
A little weather-worn,
Inspiriting habiliments
Of indigo and brown.

With specimens of song,
As if for you to choose,
Discretion in the interval,
With gay delays he goes
To some superior tree
Without a single leaf,
And shouts for joy to nobody
But his seraphic self!

IX.

AN altered look about the hills;
      A Tyrian light the village fills;
A wider sunrise in the dawn;
A deeper twilight on the lawn;
A print of a vermilion foot;
A purple finger on the slope;
A flippant fly upon the pane;
A spider at his trade again;
An added strut in chanticleer;
A flower expected everywhere;
An axe shrill singing in the woods;
Fern-odors on untravelled roads,—
All this, and more I cannot tell,
A furtive look you know as well,
And Nicodemus' mystery
Receives its annual reply.

X.

"WHOSE are the little beds," I asked,
    "Which in the valleys lie?"
Some shook their heads, and others smiled,
And no one made reply.

"Perhaps they did not hear," I said;
"I will inquire again.
Whose are the beds, the tiny beds
So thick upon the plain?"

"'T is daisy in the shortest;
A little farther on,
Nearest the door to wake the first,
Little leontodon.

"'T is iris, sir, and aster,
Anemone and bell,
Batschia in the blanket red,
And chubby daffodil."

Meanwhile at many cradles
Her busy foot she plied,
Humming the quaintest lullaby
That ever rocked a child.

"Hush! Epigea wakens!
The crocus stirs her lids,
Rhodora's cheek is crimson,–
She's dreaming of the woods."

Then, turning from them, reverent,
"Their bed-time 't is," she said;
"The bumble-bees will waken them
When April woods are red."

XI.

PIGMY seraphs gone astray,
    Velvet people from Vevay,
Belles from some lost summer day,
Bees' exclusive coterie.
Paris could not lay the fold
Belted down with emerald;
Venice could not show a cheek
Of a tint so lustrous meek.
Never such an ambuscade
As of brier and leaf displayed
For my little damask maid.
I had rather wear her grace
Than an earl's distinguished face;
I had rather dwell like her
Than be Duke of Exeter
Royalty enough for me
To subdue the bumble-bee!

XII.

To hear an oriole sing
        May be a common thing,
Or only a divine.

It is not of the bird
Who sings the same, unheard,
As unto crowd.

The fashion of the ear
Attireth that it hear
In dun or fair.

So whether it be rune,
Or whether it be none,
Is of within;

The "tune is in the tree,"
The sceptic showeth me;
"No, sir! In thee!"

XIII.

ONE of the ones that Midas touched,
        Who failed to touch us all,
Was that confiding prodigal,
The blissful oriole.

So drunk, he disavows it
With badinage divine;
So dazzling, we mistake him
For an alighting mine.

A pleader, a dissembler,
An epicure, a thief,–
Betimes an oratorio,
An ecstasy in chief;

The Jesuit of orchards,
He cheats as he enchants
Of an entire attar
For his decamping wants.

The splendor of a Burmah,
The meteor of birds,
Departing like a pageant
Of ballads and of bards.

I never thought that Jason sought
For any golden fleece;
But then I am a rural man,
With thoughts that make for peace.

But if there were a Jason,
Tradition suffer me
Behold his lost emolument
Upon the apple-tree.

XIV.

I DREADED that first robin so,
        But he is mastered now,
And I'm accustomed to him grown,–
He hurts a little, though.

I thought if I could only live
Till that first shout got by,
Not all pianos in the woods
Had power to mangle me.

I dared not meet the daffodils,
For fear their yellow gown
Would pierce me with a fashion
So foreign to my own.

I wished the grass would hurry,
So when 't was time to see,
He'd be too tall, the tallest one
Could stretch to look at me.

I could not bear the bees should come,
I wished they'd stay away
In those dim countries where they go:
What word had they for me?

They're here, though; not a creature failed,
No blossom stayed away
In gentle deference to me,
The Queen of Calvary.

Each one salutes me as he goes,
And I my childish plumes
Lift, in bereaved acknowledgment
Of their unthinking drums.

XV.

A ROUTE of evanescence
      With a revolving wheel;
A resonance of emerald,
A rush of cochineal;
And every blossom on the bush
Adjusts its tumbled head,–
The mail from Tunis, probably,
As easy morning's ride.

XVI.

THE skies can't keep their secret!
      They tell it to the hills–
The hills just tell the orchards–
And they the daffodils!

A bird, by chance, that goes that way
Soft overhead the whole.
If I should bribe the little bird,
Who knows but she would tell?

I think I won't, however,
It's finer not to know;
If summer were an axiom,
What sorcery had snow?

So keep your secret, Father!
I would not, if I could,
Know what the sapphire fellows do,
In your new-fashioned world!

XVII.

WHO robbed the woods,
  The trusting woods?
The unsuspecting trees
Brought out their burrs and mosses
His fantasy to please.
He scanned their trinkets, curious,
He grasped, he bore away.
What will the solemn hemlock,
What will the fir-tree say?

XVIII.

TWO butterflies went out at noon
  And waltzed above a stream,
Then stepped straight through the firmament
And rested on a beam;

And then together bore away
Upon a shining sea,–
Though never yet, in any port,
Their coming mentioned be.

If spoken by the distant bird,
If met in ether sea
By frigate or by merchantman,
Report was not to me.

XIX.

I STARTED early, took my dog,
  And visited the sea;
The mermaids in the basement
Came out to look at me,

And frigates in the upper floor
Extended hempen hands,
Presuming me to be a mouse
Aground, upon the sands.

But no man moved me till the tide
Went past my simple shoe,
And past my apron and my belt,
And past my bodice too,

And made as he would eat me up
As wholly as a dew
Upon a dandelion's sleeve —
And then I started too.

And he — he followed close behind;
I felt his silver heel
Upon my ankle, — then my shoes
Would overflow with pearl.

Until we met the solid town,
No man he seemed to know;
And bowing with a mighty look
At me, the sea withdrew.

XX.

ARCTURUS is his other name,—
    I'd rather call him star!
It's so unkind of science
To go and interfere!

I pull a flower from the woods,—
A monster with a glass
Computes the stamens in a breath,
And has her in a class.

Whereas I took the butterfly
Aforetime in my hat,
He sits erect in cabinets,
The clover-bells forgot.

What once was heaven, is zenith now.
Where I proposed to go
When time's brief masquerade was done,
Is mapped, and charted too!

What if the poles should frisk about
And stand upon their heads!
I hope I'm ready for the worst,
Whatever prank betides!

Perhaps the kingdom of Heaven's changed!
I hope the children there
Won't be new-fashioned when I come,
And laugh at me, and stare!

I hope the father in the skies
Will lift his little girl,—
Old-fashioned, naughty, everything,—
Over the stile of pearl!

XXI.

AN awful tempest mashed the air,
        The clouds were gaunt and few;
A black, as of a spectre's cloak,
Hid heaven and earth from view.

The creatures chuckled on the roofs
And whistled in the air,
And shook their fists and gnashed their teeth,
And swung their frenzied hair.

The morning lit, the birds arose;
The monster's faded eyes
Turned slowly to his native coast,
And peace was Paradise!

XXII.

AN everywhere of silver,
        With ropes of sand
To keep it from effacing
The track called land.

XXIII.

A BIRD came down the walk:
    He did not know I saw;
He bit an angle-worm in halves
And ate the fellow, raw.

And then he drank a dew
From a convenient grass,
And then hopped sidewise to the wall
To let a beetle pass.

He glanced with rapid eyes
That hurried all abroad,–
They looked like frightened beads, I thought;
He stirred his velvet head

Like one in danger; cautious,
I offered him a crumb,
And he unrolled his feathers
And rowed him softer home

Than oars divide the ocean,
Too silver for a seam,
Or butterflies, off banks of noon,
Leap, plashless, as they swim.

XXIV.

A NARROW fellow in the grass
      Occasionally rides;
You may have met him,–did you not,
His notice sudden is.

The grass divides as with a comb,
A spotted shaft is seen;
And then it closes at your feet
And opens further on.

He likes a boggy acre,
A floor too cool for corn.
Yet when a child, and barefoot,
I more than once, at morn,

Have passed, I thought, a whip-lash
Unbraiding in the sun,–
When, stooping to secure it,
It wrinkled, and was gone.

Several of nature's people
I know, and they know me;
I feel for them a transport
Of cordiality;

But never met this fellow,
Attended or alone,
Without a tighter breathing,
And zero at the bone.

XXV.

THE mushroom is the elf of plants,
    At evening it is not;
At morning in a truffled hut
It stops upon a spot

As if it tarried always;
And yet its whole career
Is shorter than a snake's delay,
And fleeter than a tare.

'T is vegetation's juggler,
The germ of alibi;
Doth like a bubble antedate,
And like a bubble hie.

I feel as if the grass were pleased
To have it intermit;
The surreptitious scion
Of summer's circumspect.

Had nature any outcast face,
Could she a son contemn,
Had nature an Iscariot,
That mushroom,—it is him.

XXVI.

THERE came a wind like a bugle;
⠀⠀⠀It quivered through the grass,
And a green chill upon the heat
So ominous did pass
We barred the windows and the doors
As from an emerald ghost;
The doom's electric moccason
That very instant passed.
On a strange mob of panting trees,
And fences fled away,
And rivers where the houses ran
The living looked that day.
The bell within the steeple wild
The flying tidings whirled.
How much can come
And much can go,
And yet abide the world!

XXVII.

A SPIDER sewed at night
⠀⠀⠀Without a light
Upon an arc of white.
If ruff it was of dame
Or shroud of gnome,
Himself, himself inform.
Of immortality
His strategy
Was physiognomy.

XXVIII.

I KNOW a place where summer strives
        With such a practised frost,
She each year leads her daisies back,
Recording briefly, "Lost."

But when the south wind stirs the pools
And struggles in the lanes,
Her heart misgives her for her vow,
And she pours soft refrains

Into the lap of adamant,
And spices, and the dew,
That stiffens quietly to quartz,
Upon her amber shoe.

XXIX.

THE one that could repeat the summer day
        Were greater than itself, though he
Minutest of mankind might be.
And who could reproduce the sun,
At period of going down –
The lingering and the stain, I mean –
When Orient has been outgrown,
And Occident becomes unknown,
His name remain.

XXX.

THE wind tapped like a tired man,
        And like a host, "Come in,"
I boldly answered; entered then
My residence within

A rapid, footless guest,
To offer whom a chair
Were as impossible as hand
A sofa to the air.

No bone had he to bind him,
His speech was like the push
Of numerous humming-birds at once.
From a superior bush.

His countenance a billow,
His fingers, if he pass,
Let go a music, as of tunes
Blown tremulous in glass.

He visited, still flitting;
Then, like a timid man,
Again he tapped–'t was flurriedly–
And I became alone.

XXXI.

NATURE rarer uses yellow
     Than another hue;
Saves she all of that for sunsets,–
     Prodigal of blue,

Spending scarlet like a woman,
     Yellow she affords
Only scantly and selectly,
     Like a lover's words.

XXXII.

THE leaves, like women, interchange
     Sagacious confidence;
Somewhat of nods, and somewhat of
     Portentous inference,

The parties in both cases
     Enjoining secrecy,–
Inviolable compact
     To notoriety.

XXXIII.

HOW happy is the little stone
    That rambles in the road alone,
And does n't care about careers,
And exigencies never fears;
Whose coat of elemental brown
A passing universe put on;
And independent as the sun,
Associates or glows alone,
Fulfilling absolute decree
In casual simplicity.

XXXIV.

IT sounded as if the streets were running,
    And then the streets stood still.
Eclipse was all we could see at the window,
And awe was all we could feel.

By and by the boldest stole out of his covert,
To see if time was there.
Nature was in her beryl apron,
Mixing fresher air.

XXXV.

THE rat is the concisest tenant.
     He pays no rent,–
Repudiates the obligation,
On schemes intent.

Balking our wit
To sound or circumvent,
Hate cannot harm
A foe so reticent.

Neither decree
Prohibits him,
Lawful as
Equilibrium.

XXXVI.

FREQUENTLY the woods are pink,
     Frequently are brown;
Frequently the hills undress
Behind my native town.

Oft a head is crested
I was wont to see,
And as oft a cranny
Where it used to be.

And the earth, they tell me,
On its axis turned,–
Wonderful rotation
By but twelve performed!

XXXVII.

T HE wind begun to rock the grass
        With threatening tunes and low,–
He flung a menace at the earth,
A menace at the sky.

The leaves unhooked themselves from trees
And started all abroad;
The dust did scoop itself like hands
And throw away the road.

The wagons quickened on the streets,
The thunder hurried slow;
The lightning showed a yellow beak,
And then a livid claw.

The birds put up the bars to nests,
The cattle fled to barns;
There came one drop of giant rain,
And then, as if the hands

That held the dams had parted hold,
The waters wrecked the sky,
But overlooked my father's house,
Just quartering a tree.

XXXVIII.

SOUTH winds jostle them,
    Bumblebees come,
Hover, hesitate,
Drink, and are gone.

Butterflies pause
On their passage Cashmere;
I, softly plucking,
Present them here!

XXXIX.

WHERE ships of purple gently toss
    On seas of daffodil,
Fantastic sailors mingle,
And then—the wharf is still.

XL.

SHE sweeps with many-colored brooms,
        And leaves the shreds behind;
Oh, housewife in the evening west,
Come back, and dust the pond!

You dropped a purple ravelling in,
You dropped an amber thread;
And now you've littered all the East
With duds of emerald!

And still she plies her spotted brooms,
And still the aprons fly,
Till brooms fade softly into stars—
And then I come away.

XLI.

LIKE mighty footlights burned the red
        At bases of the trees,—
The far theatricals of day
Exhibiting to these.

'T was universe that did applaud
While, chiefest of the crowd,
Enabled by his royal dress,
Myself distinguished God.

XLII.

BRING me the sunset in a cup,
　　Reckon the morning's flagons up,
　And say how many dew;
Tell me how far the morning leaps,
Tell me what time the weaver sleeps
　Who spun the breadths of blue!

Write me how many notes there be
In the new robin's ecstasy
　Among astonished boughs;
How many trips the tortoise makes,
How many cups the bee partakes,—
　The debauchee of dews!

Also, who laid the rainbow's piers,
Also, who leads the docile spheres
　By withes of supple blue?
Whose fingers string the stalactite,
Who counts the wampum of the night,
　To see that none is due?

Who built this little Alban house
And shut the windows down so close
　My spirit cannot see?
Who 'll let me out some gala day,
Wit implements to fly away,
　Passing pomposity?

XLIII.

BLAZING in gold and quenching in purple,
        Leaping like leopards to the sky,
Then at the feet of the old horizon
Laying her spotted face, to die;

Stooping as low as the otter's window,
Touching the roof and tinting the barn,
Kissing her bonnet to the meadow,–
And the juggler of day is gone!

XLIV.

FARTHER in summer than the birds,
        Pathetic from the grass,
A minor nation celebrates
Its unobtrusive mass.

No ordinance is seen,
So gradual the grace,
A pensive custom it becomes,
Enlarging loneliness.

Antiquest felt at noon
When August, burning low,
Calls forth this spectral canticle,
Repose to typify.

Remit as yet no grace,
No furrow on the glow,
Yet a druidic difference
Enhances nature now.

XLV.

As imperceptibly as grief
    The summer lapsed away,–
Too imperceptible, at last,
To seem like perfidy.

A quietness distilled,
As twilight long begun,
Or Nature, spending with herself
Sequestered afternoon.

The dusk drew earlier in,
The morning foreign shone,–
A courteous, yet harrowing grace,
As guest who would be gone.

And thus, without a wing,
Or service of a keel,
Our summer made her light escape
Into the beautiful.

XLVI.

It can't be summer,–that got through;
    It's early yet for spring;
There's that long town of white to cross
Before the blackbirds sing.

It can't be dying,–it's too rouge,–
The dead shall go in white.
So sunset shuts my question down
With clasps of chrysolite.

XLVII.

THE gentian weaves her fringes,
        The maple's loom is red.
My departing blossoms
Obviate parade.

A brief, but patient illness,
An hour to prepare;
And one, below this morning,
Is where the angels are.

It was a short procession,–
The bobolink was there,
An aged bee addressed us,
And then we knelt in prayer.

We trust that she was willing,–
We ask that we may be.
Summer, sister, seraph,
Let us go with thee!

In the name of the bee
And of the butterfly
And of the breeze, amen!

XLVIII.

GOD made a little gentian;
        It tried to be a rose
And failed, and all the summer laughed.
But just before the snows
There came a purple creature
That ravished all the hill;
And summer hid her forehead,
And mockery was still.
The frosts were her condition;
The Tyrian would not come
Until the North evoked it.
"Creator! shall I bloom?"

XLIX.

BESIDES the autumn poets sing,
        A few prosaic days
A little this side of the snow
And that side of the haze.

A few incisive mornings,
A few ascetic eves,—
Gone Mr. Bryant's golden-rod,
And Mr. Thomson's sheaves.

Still is the bustle in the brook,
Sealed are the spicy valves;
Mesmeric fingers softly touch
The eyes of many elves.

Perhaps a squirrel may remain,
My sentiments to share.
Grant me, O Lord, a sunny mind,
Thy windy will to bear!

L.

IT sifts from leaden sieves,
      It powders all the wood,
It fills with alabaster wool
The wrinkles of the road.

It makes an even face
Of mountain and of plain,–
Unbroken forehead from the east
Unto the east again.

It reaches to the fence,
It wraps it, rail by rail,
Till it is lost in fleeces;
It flings a crystal veil

On stump and stack and stem,–
The summer's empty room,
Acres of seams where harvests were,
Recordless, but for them.

It ruffles wrists of posts,
As ankles of a queen,–
Then stills its artisans like ghosts,
Denying they have been.

LI.

NO brigadier throughout the year
     So civic as the jay.
A neighbor and a warrior too,
With shrill felicity

Pursuing winds that censure us
A February day,
The brother of the universe
Was never blown away.

The snow and he are intimate;
I've often seen them play
When heaven looked upon us all
With such severity,

I felt apology were due
To an insulted sky,
Whose pompous frown was nutriment
To their temerity.

The pillow of this daring head
Is pungent evergreens;
His larder—terse and militant—
Unknown, refreshing things;

His character a tonic,
His future a dispute;
Unfair an immortality
That leaves this neighbor out.

IV. TIME AND ETERNITY

I.

LET down the bars, O Death!
    The tired flocks come in
Whose bleating ceases to repeat,
Whose wandering is done.

Thine is the stillest night,
Thine the securest fold;
Too near thou art for seeking thee,
Too tender to be told.

II.

GOING to heaven!
        I don't know when,
Pray do not ask me how,–
Indeed, I'm too astonished
To think of answering you!
Going to heaven!–
How dim it sounds!
And yet it will be done
As sure as flocks go home at night
Unto the shepherd's arm!

Perhaps you're going too!
Who knows?
If you should get there first,
Save just a little place for me
Close to the two I lost!
The smallest "robe" will fit me,
And just a bit of "crown;"
For you know we do not mind our dress
When we are going home.

I'm glad I don't believe it,
For it would stop my breath,
And I'd like to look a little more
At such a curious earth!
I am glad they did believe it
Whom I have never found
Since the mighty autumn afternoon
I left them in the ground.

III.

AT least to pray is left, is left.
       O Jesus! in the air
I know not which thy chamber is,–
I'm knocking everywhere.

Thou stirrest earthquake in the South,
And maelstrom in the sea;
Say, Jesus Christ of Nazareth,
Hast thou no arm for me?

IV.

STEP lightly on this narrow spot!
       The broadest land that grows
Is not so ample as the breast
These emerald seams enclose.

Step lofty; for this name is told
As far as cannon dwell,
Or flag subsist, or fame export
Her deathless syllable.

V.

MORNS like these we parted;
    Noons like these she rose,
Fluttering first, then firmer,
To her fair repose.

Never did she lisp it,
And 't was not for me;
She was mute from transport,
I, from agony!

Till the evening, nearing,
One the shutters drew—
Quick! a sharper rustling!
And this linnet flew!

VI.

A DEATH-BLOW is a life-blow to some
    Who, till they died, did not alive become;
Who, had they lived, and died, but when
They died, vitality begun.

VII.

I READ my sentence steadily,
  Reviewed it with my eyes,
To see that I made no mistake
In its extremest clause,–

The date, and manner of the shame;
And then the pious form
That "God have mercy" on the soul
The jury voted him.

I made my soul familiar
With her extremity,
That at the last it should not be
A novel agony,

But she and Death, acquainted,
Meet tranquilly as friends,
Salute and pass without a hint,–
And there the matter ends.

VIII.

I HAVE not told my garden yet,
        Lest that should conquer me;
I have not quite the strength now
To break it to the bee.

I will not name it in the street,
For shops would stare, that I,
So shy, so very ignorant,
Should have the face to die.

The hillsides must not know it,
Where I have rambled so,
Nor tell the loving forests
The day that I shall go,

Nor lisp it at the table,
Nor heedless by the way
Hint that within the riddle
One will walk to-day!

IX.

They dropped like flakes, they dropped like stars,
      Like petals from a rose,
When suddenly across the June
   A wind with fingers goes.

They perished in the seamless grass,—
   No eye could find the place;
But God on his repealless list
   Can summon every face.

X.

THE only ghost I ever saw
      Was dressed in mechlin,—so;
He wore no sandal on his foot,
And stepped like flakes of snow.
His gait was soundless, like the bird,
But rapid, like the roe;
His fashions quaint, mosaic,
Or, haply, mistletoe.

His conversation seldom,
His laughter like the breeze
That dies away in dimples
Among the pensive trees.
Our interview was transient,—
Of me, himself was shy;
And God forbid I look behind
Since that appalling day!

XI.

SOME, too fragile for winter winds,
        The thoughtful grave encloses,–
Tenderly tucking them in from frost
Before their feet are cold.

Never the treasures in her nest
The cautious grave exposes,
Building where schoolboy dare not look
And sportsman is not bold.

This covert have all the children
Early aged, and often cold,–
Sparrows unnoticed by the Father;
Lambs for whom time had not a fold.

XII.

AS by the dead we love to sit,
        Become so wondrous dear,
As for the lost we grapple,
Though all the rest are here,–

In broken mathematics
We estimate our prize,
Vast, in its fading ratio,
To our penurious eyes!

XIII.

DEATH sets a thing significant
        The eye had hurried by,
Except a perished creature
Entreat us tenderly

To ponder little workmanships
In crayon or in wool,
With "This was last her fingers did,"
Industrious until

The thimble weighed too heavy,
The stitches stopped themselves,
And then 't was put among the dust
Upon the closet shelves.

A book I have, a friend gave,
Whose pencil, here and there,
Had notched the place that pleased him,–
At rest his fingers are.

Now, when I read, I read not,
For interrupting tears
Obliterate the etchings
Too costly for repairs.

XIV.

I WENT to heaven,—
   'T was a small town,
Lit with a ruby,
Lathed with down.
Stiller than the fields
At the full dew,
Beautiful as pictures
No man drew.
People like the moth,
Of mechlin, frames,
Duties of gossamer,
And eider names.
Almost contented
I could be
'Mong such unique
Society.

XV.

THEIR height in heaven comforts not,
       Their glory nought to me;
'Twas best imperfect, as it was;
I'm finite, I can't see.

The house of supposition,
The glimmering frontier
The skirts the acres of perhaps,
To me shows insecure.

The wealth I had contented me;
If't was a meaner size,
Then I had counted it until
It pleased my narrow eyes

Better than larger values,
However true their show;
This timid life of evidence
Keeps pleading, "I don't know."

XVI.

THERE is a shame of nobleness
       Confronting sudden pelf,–
A finer shame of ecstasy
Convicted of itself.

A best disgrace a brave man feels,
Acknowledged of the brave,–
One more "Ye Blessed" to be told;
But this involves the grave.

XVII.

TRIUMPH may be of several kinds.
        There's triumph in the room
When that old imperator, Death,
By faith is overcome.

There's triumph of the finer mind
When truth, affronted long,
Advances calm to her supreme,
Her God her only throng.

A triumph when temptation's bribe
Is slowly handed back,
One eye upon the heaven renounced
And one upon the rack.

Severer triumph, by himself
Experienced, who can pass
Acquitted from that naked bar,
Jehovah's countenance!

XVIII.

POMPLESS no life can pass away;
    The lowliest career
To the same pageant wends its way
    As that exalted here.
How cordial is the mystery!
    The hospitable pall
A "this way" beckons spaciously,–
    A miracle for all!

XIX.

I NOTICED people disappeared,
    When but a little child,–
Supposed they visited remote,
Or settled regions wild.

Now know I they both visited
And settled regions wild,
But did because they died,–a fact
Withheld the little child!

XX.

I HAD no cause to be awake,
      My best was gone to sleep,
And morn a new politeness took,
And failed to wake them up,

But called the others clear,
And passed their curtains by.
Sweet morning, when I over-sleep,
Knock, recollect, for me!

I looked at sunrise once,
And then I looked at them,
At wishfulness in me arose
For circumstance the same.

'T was such an ample peace,
It could not hold a sigh,–
'T was Sabbath with the bells divorced,
'T was sunset all the day.

So choosing but a gown
And taking but a prayer,
The only raiment I should need,
I struggled, and was there.

XXI.

IF anybody's friend be dead,
        It's sharpest of the theme
The thinking how they walked alive,
At such and such a time.

Their costume, of a Sunday,
Some manner of the hair,–
A prank nobody knew but them,
Lost, in the sepulchre.

How warm they were on such a day:
You almost feel the date,
So short way off it seems; and now,
They're centuries from that.

How pleased they were at what you said;
You try to touch the smile,
And dip your fingers in the frost:
When was it, can you tell,

You asked the company to tea,
Acquaintance, just a few,
And chatted close with this grand thing
That don't remember you?

Past bows and invitations,
Past interview, and vow,
Past what ourselves can estimate,–
That makes the quick of woe!

XXII.

OUR journey had advanced;
        Our feet were almost come
To that odd fork in Being's road,
Eternity by term.

Our pace took sudden awe,
Our feet reluctant led.
Before were cities, but between,
The forest of the dead.

Retreat was out of hope,—
Behind, a sealed route,
Eternity's white flag before,
And God at every gate.

XXIII.

AMPLE make this bed.
        Make this bed with awe;
In it wait till judgment break
Excellent and fair.

Be its mattress straight,
Be its pillow round;
Let no sunrise's yellow noise
Interrupt this ground.

XXIV.

ON such a night, or such a night,
        Would anybody care
Of such a little figure
Slipped quiet from its chair,

So quiet, oh, how quiet!
That nobody might know
But that the little figure
Rocked softer, to and fro?

On such a dawn, or such a dawn,
Would anybody sigh
That such a little figure
Too sound asleep did lie

For chanticleer to wake it,–
Or stirring house below,
Or giddy bird in orchard,
Or early task to do?

There was a little figure plump
For every little knoll,
Busy needles, and spools of thread,
And trudging feet from school.

Playmates, and holidays, and nuts,
And visions vast and small.
Strange that the feet so precious charged
Should reach so small a goal!

XXV.

ESSENTIAL oils are wrung:
    The attar from the rose
Is not expressed by suns alone,
It is the gift of screws.

The general rose decays;
But this, in lady's drawer,
Makes summer when the lady lies
In ceaseless rosemary.

XXVI.

I LIVED on dread; to those who know
    The stimulus there is
In danger, other impetus
Is numb and vital-less.

As 't were a spur upon the soul,
A fear will urge it where
To go without the spectre's aid
Were challenging despair.

XXVII.

IF I should die,
          And you should live,
And time should gurgle on,
And morn should beam,
And noon should burn,
As it has usual done;
If birds should build as early,
And bees as bustling go,–
One might depart at option
From enterprise below!
'T is sweet to know that stocks will stand
When we with daisies lie,
That commerce will continue,
And trades as briskly fly.
It makes the parting tranquil
And keeps the soul serene,
That gentlemen so sprightly
Conduct the pleasing scene!

XXVIII.

HER final summer was it,
        And yet we guessed it not;
If tenderer industriousness
Pervaded her, we thought

A further force of life
Developed from within,–
When Death lit all the shortness up,
And made the hurry plain.

We wondered at our blindness,–
When nothing was to see
But her Carrara guide-post,–
At our stupidity,

When, duller than our dulness,
The busy darling lay,
So busy was she, finishing,
So leisurely were we!

XXIX.

ONE need not be a chamber to be haunted,
    One need not be a house;
The brain has corridors surpassing
Material place.

Far safer, of a midnight meeting
External ghost,
Than an interior confronting
That whiter host.

Far safer through an Abbey gallop,
The stones achase,
Than, moonless, one's own self encounter
In lonesome place.

Ourself, behind ourself concealed,
Should startle most;
Assassin, hid in our apartment,
Be horror's least.

The prudent carries a revolver,
He bolts the door,
O'erlooking a superior spectre
More near.

XXX.

SHE died,–this was the way she died;
        And when her breath was done,
Took up her simple wardrobe
And started for the sun.

Her little figure at the gate
The angels must have spied,
Since I could never find her
Upon the mortal side.

XXXI.

WAIT till the majesty of Death
        Invests so mean a brow!
Almost a powdered footman
Might dare to touch it now!

Wait till in everlasting robes
This democrat is dressed,
Then prate about "preferment"
And "station" and the rest!

Around this quiet courtier
Obsequious angels wait!
Full royal is his retinue,
Full purple is his state!

A lord might dare to lift the hat
To such a modest clay,
Since that my Lord, "the Lord of lords"
Receives unblushingly!

XXXII.

WENT up a year this evening!
    I recollect it well!
Amid no bells nor bravos
    The bystanders will tell!
Cheerful, as to the village,
    Tranquil, as to repose,
Chastened, as to the chapel,
    This humble tourist rose.
Did not talk of returning,
    Alluded to no time
When, were the gales propitious,
    We might look for him;
Was grateful for the roses
    In life's diverse bouquet,
Talked softly of new species
    To pick another day.
Beguiling thus the wonder,
    The wondrous nearer drew;
Hands bustled at the moorings—
    The crowd respectful grew.
Ascended from our vision
    To countenances new!
A difference, a daisy,
    Is all the rest I knew!

XXXIII.

TAKEN from men this morning,
       Carried by men to-day,
Met by the gods with banners
Who marshalled her away.

One little maid from playmates,
One little mind from school,–
There must be guests in Eden;
All the rooms are full.

Far as the east from even,
Dim as the border star,–
Courtiers quaint, in kingdoms,
Our departed are.

XXXIV.

WHAT inn is this
       Where for the night
Peculiar traveller comes?
Who is the landlord?
Where the maids?
Behold, what curious rooms!
No ruddy fires on the hearth,
No brimming tankards flow.
Necromancer, landlord,
Who are these below?

XXXV.

IT was not death, for I stood up,
        And all the dead lie down;
It was not night, for all the bells
Put out their tongues, for noon.

It was not frost, for on my flesh
I felt siroccos crawl,—
Nor fire, for just my marble feet
Could keep a chancel cool.

And yet it tasted like them all;
The figures I have seen
Set orderly, for burial,
Reminded me of mine,

As if my life were shaven
And fitted to a frame,
And could not breathe without a key;
And 't was like midnight, some,

When everything that ticked has stopped,
And space stares, all around,
Or grisly frosts, first autumn morns,
Repeal the beating ground.

But most like chaos,—stopless, cool,—
Without a chance or spar,
Or even a report of land
To justify despair.

XXXVI.

I SHOULD not dare to leave my friend,
Because – because if he should die
While I was gone, and I – too late –
Should reach the heart that wanted me;

If I should disappoint the eyes
That hunted, hunted so, to see,
And could not bear to shut until
They "noticed" me – they noticed me;

If I should stab the patient faith
So sure I'd come – so sure I'd come,
It listening, listening, went to sleep
Telling my tardy name, –

My heart would wish it broke before,
Since breaking then, since breaking then,
Were useless as next morning's sun,
Where midnight frosts had lain!

XXXVII.

GREAT streets of silence led away
        To neighborhoods of pause;
Here was no notice, no dissent,
No universe, no laws.

By clocks 't was morning, and for night
The bells at distance called;
But epoch had no basis here,
For period exhaled.

XXXVIII.

A THROE upon the features
        A hurry in the breath,
An ecstasy of parting
Denominated "Death,"–

An anguish at the mention,
Which, when to patience grown,
I've known permission given
To rejoin its own.

XXXIX.

OF tribulation these are they
          Denoted by the white;
The spangled gowns, a lesser rand
Of victors designate.

All these did conquer; but the ones
Who overcame most times
Wear nothing commoner than snow,
No ornament but palms.

Surrender is a sort unknown
On this superior soil;
Defeat, an outgrown anguish,
Remembered as the mile

Our panting ankle barely gained
When night devoured the road;
But we stood whispering in the house,
And all we said was "Saved"!

XL.

I THINK just how my shape will rise
    When I shall be forgiven,
Till hair and eyes and timid head
Are out of sight, in heaven.

I think just how my lips will weigh
With shapeless, quivering prayer
That you, so late, consider me,
The sparrow of your care.

I mind me that of anguish sent,
Some drifts were moved away
Before my simple bosom broke,–
And why not this, if they?

And so, until delirious borne
I con that thing,–"forgiven,"–
Till with long fright and longer trust
I drop my heart, unshriven!

XLI.

AFTER a hundred years
        Nobody knows the place,–
Agony, that enacted there,
Motionless as peace.

Weeds triumphant ranged.
Strangers strolled and spelled
At the lone orthography
Of the elder dead.

Winds of summer fields
Recollect the way,–
Instinct picking up the key
Dropped by memory.

XLII.

LAY this laurel on the one
        Too intrinsic for renown.
Laurel! veil your deathless tree,–
Him you chasten, that is he!

. . .

POEMS

BY

EMILY DICKINSON

· *THIRD SERIES* ·

. . .

PRELUDE

It's all I have to bring to-day
This, and my heart beside,
This and my heart, and all the fields,
And all the meadows wide.
Be sure you count, should I forget,—
Some one the sum could tell,—
This, and my heart, and all the bees
Which in the clover dwell.

. . .

PREFACE

THE intellectual activity of Emily Dickinson was so great that a large and characteristic choice is still possible among her literary material, and this third volume of her verses is put forth in response to the repeated wish of the admirers of her peculiar genius.

Much of Emily Dickinson's prose was rhythmic,—even rhymed, though frequently not set apart in lines. Also many verses, written as such, were sent to friends in letters; these were published in 1894, in the volumes of her *Letters*. It has not been necessary, however, to include them in this Series, and all have been omitted, except three or four exceptionally strong ones, as ["There is no frigate like a book"] and ["If recollecting were forgetting. . ."].

There is internal evidence that many of the poems were simply spontaneous flashes of insight, apparently unrelated to outward circumstance. Others, however, had an obvious personal origin; for example, the verses "I had a Guinea golden," which seem to have been sent to some friend travelling in Europe, as a dainty reminder of letter-writing delinquencies. The surroundings in which any of Emily Dickinson's verses are known to have been written usually serve to explain them clearly; but in general the present volume is full of thoughts needing no interpretation to those who apprehend this scintillating spirit.

M.L.T.

AMHERST, *October,* 1896

I. Life

I.

'TIS little I could care for pearls
    Who own the ample sea;
Or brooches, when the Emperor
    With rubies pelteth me;

Or gold, who am the Prince of Mines;
    Or diamonds, when I see
A diadem to fit a dome
Continual crowning me.

II.

SUPERIORITY to fate
    Is difficult to learn.
'T is not conferred by any,
    But possible to earn

A pittance at a time,
    Until, to her surprise,
The soul with strict economy
    Subsists till Paradise.

III.

HOPE is a subtle glutton;
    He feeds upon the fair;
And yet, inspected closely,
    What abstinence is there!

His is the halcyon table
    That never seats but one,
And whatsoever is consumed
    The same amounts remain.

IV.

FORBIDDEN fruit a flavor has
    That lawful orchards mocks;
How luscious lies the pea within
    The pod that Duty locks!

V.

HEAVEN is what I cannot reach!
        The apple on the tree,
Provided it do hopeless hang,
    That "heaven" is, to me.

The color on the cruising cloud,
    The interdicted ground
Behind the hill, the house
behind,—
    There Paradise is found!

VI.

A WORD is dead
        When it is said,
        Some say.
    I say it just
    Begins to live
        That day.

VII.

TO venerate the simple days
        Which lead the seasons by,
Needs but to remember
    That from you or me
They take the trifle
    Termed mortality!

To invest existence with a stately air,
Needs but to remember
    That the acorn there
Is the egg of forests
    For the upper air!

VIII.

IT'S such a little thing to weep,
        So short a thing to sigh;
And yet by trades the size of these
    We men and women die!

IX.

DROWNING is not so pitiful
        As the attempt to rise.
Three times, 't is said, a sinking man
        Comes up to face the skies,
And then declines forever
        To that abhorred abode
Where hope and he part company,–
        For he is grasped of God.
The Maker's cordial visage,
        However good to see,
Is shunned, we must admit it,
        Like an adversity.

X.

HOW still the bells in steeples stand,
        Till, swollen with the sky,
They leap upon their silver feet
        In frantic melody!

XI.

IF the foolish call them "flowers,"
    Need the wiser tell?
If the savans "classify" them,
    It is just as well!

Those who read the *Revelations*
    Must not criticise
Those who read the same edition
    With beclouded eyes!

Could we stand with that old Moses
    Canaan denied,—
Scan, like him, the stately landscape
    On the other side,—

Doubtless we should deem superfluous
    Many sciences
Not pursued by learned angels
    In scholastic skies!

Low amid that glad *Belles lettres*
    Grant that we may stand,
Stars, amid profound Galaxies,
    At that grand "Right hand"!

XII.

COULD mortal lip divine
　　　The undeveloped freight
Of a delivered syllable,
　　　'T would crumble with the weight.

XIII.

MY life closed twice before its close;
　　　It yet remains to see
If Immortality unveil
　　　A third event to me,

So huge, so hopeless to conceive,
　　　As these that twice befell.
Parting is all we know of heaven,
　　　And all we need of hell.

XIV.

WE never know how high we are
　　　Till we are called to rise;
And then, if we are true to plan,
　　　Our statures touch the skies.

The heroism we recite
　　　Would be a daily thing,
Did not ourselves the cubits warp
　　　For fear to be a king.

XV.

WHILE I was fearing it, it came,
 But came with less of fear,
Because that fearing it so long
 Had almost made it dear.
There is a fitting a dismay,
 A fitting a despair.
'T is harder knowing it is due,
 Than knowing it is here.
The trying on the utmost,
 The morning it is new,
Is terribler than wearing it
 A whole existence through.

XVI.

THERE is no frigate like a book
 To take us lands away,
Nor any coursers like a page
 Of prancing poetry.
This traverse may the poorest take
 Without oppress of toll:
How frugal is the chariot
 That bears a human soul!

XVII.

WHO has not found the heaven below
    Will fail of it above.
God's residence is next to mine,
    His furniture is love.

XVIII.

A FACE devoid of love or grace,
    A hateful, hard, successful face,
  A face with which a stone
Would feel as thoroughly at ease
As were they old acquaintances,—
    First time together thrown.

XIX.

I HAD a guinea golden;
    I lost it in the sand,
And though the sum was simple,
    And pounds were in the land,
Still had it such a value
    Unto my frugal eye,
That when I could not find it
    I sat me down to sigh.

I had a crimson robin
    Who sang full many a day,
But when the woods were painted
    He, too, did fly away.
Time brought me other robins,–
    Their ballads were the same,–
Still for my missing troubadour
    I kept the "house at hame."

I had a star in heaven;
    One Pleiad was its name,
And when I was not heeding
    It wandered from the same.
And though the skies are crowded,
    And all the night ashine,
I do not care about it,
    Since none of them are mine.

My story has a moral;
    I have a missing friend,–
Pleiad its name, and robin,
    And guinea in the sand,–
And when this mournful ditty,
    Accompanied with tear,

Shall meet the eye of traitor
    In country far from here,
Grant that repentance solemn
    May seize upon his mind,
And he no consolation
    Beneath the sun may find.

XX.

FROM all the jails the boys and girls
        Ecstatically leap,–
Beloved, only afternoon
    That prison doesn't keep.

They storm the earth and stun the
air,
    A mob of solid bliss.
Alas! that frowns could lie in wait
    For such a foe as this!

XXI.

FEW get enough,– enough is one;
      To that ethereal throng
Have not each one of us the right
      To stealthily belong?

XXII.

UPON the gallows hung a wretch,
      Too sullied for the hell
To which the law entitled him.
      As nature's curtain fell
The one who bore him tottered in,
      For this was woman's son.
"'T was all I had," she stricken gasped;
      Oh, what a livid boon!

XXIII.

I FELT a clearing in my mind
        As if my brain had split;
I tried to match it, seam by seam,
        But could not make them fit.

The thought behind I strove to join
        Unto the thought before,
But sequence ravelled out of reach
        Like balls upon a floor.

XXIV.

THE reticent volcano keeps
        His never slumbering plan;
Confided are his projects pink
        To no precarious man.

If nature will not tell the tale
        Jehovah told to her,
Can human nature not survive
        Without a listener?

Admonished by her buckled lips
        Let every babbler be.
The only secret people keep
        Is Immortality.

XXV.

IF recollecting were forgetting,
    Then I remember not;
And if forgetting, recollecting,
    How near I had forgot!
And if to miss were merry,
    And if to mourn were gay,
How very blithe the fingers
    That gathered these to-day!

XXVI.

THE farthest thunder that I heard
    Was nearer than the sky,
And rumbles still, though torrid noons
    Have lain their missiles by.
The lightning that preceded it
    Struck no one but myself,
But I would not exchange the bolt
    For all the rest of life.
Indebtedness to oxygen
    The chemist may repay,
But not the obligation
    To electricity.
It founds the homes and decks the days,
    And every clamor bright
Is but the gleam concomitant
    Of that waylaying light.
The thought is quiet as a flake,—
    A crash without a sound;
How life's reverberation
    Its explanation found!

XXVII.

ON the bleakness of my lot
  Bloom I strove to raise.
Late, my acre of a rock
  Yielded grape and maize.

Soil of flint if steadfast tilled
  Will reward the hand;
Seed of palm by Lybian sun
  Fructified in sand.

XXVIII.

A DOOR just opened on a street—
  I, lost, was passing by—
An instant's width of warmth
disclosed,
  And wealth, and company.

The door as sudden shut, and I,
  I, lost, was passing by,—
Lost doubly, but by contrast most,
  Enlightening misery.

XXIX.

ARE friends delight or pain?
        Could bounty but remain
Riches were good.

But if they only stay
Bolder to fly away,
        Riches are sad.

XXX.

ASHES denote that fire was;
        Respect the grayest pile
For the departed creature's sake
That hovered there awhile.

Fire exists the first in light,
        And then consolidates,–
Only the chemist can disclose
Into what carbonates.

XXXI.

FATE slew him, but he did not drop;
　　She felled—he did not fall—
Impaled him on her fiercest stakes—
He neutralized them all.

She stung him, sapped his firm advance,
　　But, when her worst was done,
And he, unmoved, regarded her,
Acknowledged him a man.

XXXII.

FINITE to fail, but infinite to venture.
　　For the one ship that struts the shore
Many's the gallant, overwhelmed creature
Nodding in navies nevermore.

XXXIII.

I MEASURE every grief I meet
   With analytic eyes;
I wonder if it weighs like mine,
   Or has an easier size.

I wonder if they bore it long,
   Or did it just begin?
I could not tell the date of mine,
   It feels so old a pain.

I wonder if it hurts to live,
   And if they have to try,
And whether, could they choose between,
   They would not rather die.

I wonder if when years have piled—
   Some thousands—on the cause
Of early hurt, if such a lapse
   Could give them any pause;

Or would they go on aching still
   Through centuries above,
Enlightened to a larger pain
   By contrast with the love.

The grieved are many, I am told;
   The reason deeper lies,—
Death is but one and comes but once,
   And only nails the eyes.

There's grief of want, and grief of cold,–
   A sort they call "despair";
There's banishment from native eyes,
   In sight of native air.

And though I may not guess the kind
   Correctly, yet to me
A piercing comfort it affords
   In passing Calvary,

To note the fashions of the cross,
   Of those that stand alone,
Still fascinated to presume
   That some are like my own.

XXXIV.

I HAVE a king who does not speak;
   So, wondering, thro' the hours meek
   I trudge the day away,–
Half glad when it is night and sleep,
If, haply, thro' a dream to peep
   In parlors shut by day.

And if I do, when morning comes,
It is as if a hundred drums
   Did round my pillow roll,
And shouts fill all my childish sky,
And bells keep saying "victory"
   From steeples in my soul!

And if I don't, the little Bird
Within the Orchard is not heard,
    And I omit to pray,
"Father, thy will be done" to-day,
For my will goes the other way,
    And it were perjury!

XXXV.

IT dropped so low in my regard
    I heard it hit the ground,
And go to pieces on the stones
    At bottom of my mind;

Yet blamed the fate that fractured, less
    Than I reviled myself
For entertaining plated wares
    Upon my silver shelf.

XXXVI.

TO lose one's faith surpasses
        The loss of an estate,
Because estates can be
        Replenished,—faith cannot.

Inherited with life,
        Belief but once can be;
Annihilate a single clause,
        And Being's beggary.

XXXVII.

I HAD a daily bliss
        I half indifferent viewed,
Till sudden I perceived it stir,—
        It grew as I pursued,

Till when, around a crag,
        It wasted from my sight,
Enlarged beyond my utmost scope,
        I learned its sweetness right.

XXXVIII.

I WORKED for chaff, and earning wheat
    Was haughty and betrayed.
What right had fields to arbitrate
  In matters ratified?

I tasted wheat,–and hated chaff,
  And thanked the ample friend;
Wisdom is more becoming viewed
  At distance than at hand.

XXXIX.

LIFE, and Death, and Giants
    Such as these, are still.
Minor apparatus, hopper of the mill,
Beetle at the candle,
  Or a fife's small fame,
Maintain by accident
  That they proclaim.

XL.

OUR lives are Swiss,—
        So still, so cool,
Till, some odd afternoon,
The Alps neglect their curtains,
        And we look farther on.

Italy stands the other side,
        While, like a guard between,
The solemn Alps,
The siren Alps,
        Forever intervene!

XLI.

REMEMBRANCE has a rear and front,—
        'T is something like a house;
It has a garret also
        For refuse and the mouse.

Besides, the deepest cellar
        That ever mason hewed;
Look to it, by its fathoms
        Ourselves be not pursued.

XLII.

TO hand our head ostensibly,
    And subsequent to find
That such was not the posture
    Of our immortal mind,

Affords the sly presumption
    That, in so dense a fuzz,
You, too, take cobweb attitudes
    Upon a plane of gauze!

XLIII.

THE brain is wider than the sky,
    For, put them side by side,
The one the other will include
    With ease, and you beside.

The brain is deeper than the sea,
    For, hold them, blue to blue,
The one the other will absorb,
    As sponges, buckets do.

The brain is just the weight of God,
    For, lift them, pound for pound,
And they will differ, if they do,
    As syllable from sound.

XLIV.

THE bone that has no marrow;
    What ultimate for that?
It is not fit for table,
    For beggar, or for cat.

A bone has obligations,
    A being has the same;
A marrowless assembly
    Is culpabler than shame.

But how shall finished creatures
    A function fresh obtain?—
Old Nicodemus' phantom
    Confronting us again!

XLV.

THE past is such a curious creature,
    To look her in the face
A transport may reward us,
    Or a disgrace.

Unarmed if any meet her,
    I charge him, fly!
Her rusty ammunition
    Might yet reply!

XLVI.

TO help our bleaker parts
        Salubrious hours are given,
Which if they do not fit for earth
    Drill silently for heaven.

XLVII.

WHAT soft, cherubic creatures
        These gentlewomen are!
One would as soon assault a plush
    Or violate a star.

Such dimity convictions,
    A horror so refined
Of freckled human nature,
    Of Deity ashamed,—

It's such a common glory,
    A fisherman's degree!
Redemption, brittle lady,
    Be so, ashamed of thee.

XLVIII.

WHO never wanted,–maddest joy
    Remains to him unknown:
The banquet of abstemiousness
    Surpasses that of wine.

Within its hope, though yet ungrasped
    Desire's perfect goal,
No nearer, lest reality
    Should disenthrall thy soul.

XLIX.

IT might be easier
    To fail with land in sight,
Than gain by blue peninsula
    To perish of delight.

L.

YOU cannot put a fire out;
    A thing that can ignite
Can go, itself, without a fan
    Upon the slowest night.

You cannot fold a flood
    And put it in a drawer,–
Because the winds would find it out,
    And tell your cedar floor.

LI.

A MODEST lot, a fame *petite,*
    A brief campaign of sting and sweet
Is plenty! Is enough!
A sailor's business is the shore,
    A soldier's—balls. Who asketh more
Must seek the neighboring life!

LII.

IS bliss, then, such abyss
    I must not put my foot amiss
For fear I spoil my shoe?

I'd rather suit my foot
Than save my boot,
For yet to buy another pair
Is possible
At any fair.

But bliss is sold just once;
The patent lost
None buy it any more.

LIII.

I STEPPED from plank to plank
        So slow and cautiously;
The stars about my head I felt,
    About my feet the sea.

I knew not but the next
    Would be my final inch,–
This gave me that precarious gait
    Some call experience.

LIV.

ONE day is there of the series
        Termed Thanksgiving day,
Celebrated part at table,
    Part in memory.

Neither patriarch nor pussy,
    I dissect the play;
Seems it, to my hooded thinking,
    Reflex holiday.

Had there been no sharp subtraction
    From the early sum,
Not an acre or a caption
    Where was once a room,

Not a mention, whose small pebble
    Wrinkled any bay,–
Unto such, were such assembly,
    'T were Thanksgiving day.

LV.

SOFTENED by Time's consummate plush,
  How sleek the woe appears
That threatened childhood's citadel
And undermined the years!

Bisected now by bleaker griefs,
  We envy the despair
That devastated childhood's realm,
  So easy to repair.

II. LOVE

I.

PROUD of my broken heart since thou didst break it,
  Proud of the pain I did not feel till thee,
Proud of my night since thou with moons dost slake it,
  Not to partake thy passion, my humility.

II.

MY worthiness is all my doubt,
  His merit all my fear,
Contrasting which, my qualities
  Do lowlier appear;

Lest I should insufficient prove
  For his beloved need,
The chiefest apprehension
  Within my loving creed.

So I, the undivine abode
  Of his elect content,
Conform my soul as 't were a church
  Unto her sacrament.

III.

LOVE is anterior to life,
    Posterior to death,
Initial of creation, and
    The exponent of breath.

IV.

ONE blessing had I, than the rest
    So larger to my eyes
That I stopped gauging, satisfied,
    For this enchanted size.

It was the limit of my dream,
    The focus of my prayer,—
A perfect, paralyzing bliss
    Contented as despair.

I knew no more of want or cold,
    Phantasms both become,
For this new value in the soul,
    Supremest earthly sum.

The heaven below the heaven above
    Obscured with ruddier hue.
Life's latitude leant over-full;
    The judgment perished, too.

Why joys so scantily disburse,
    Why Paradise defer,
Why floods are served to us in bowls,—
    I speculate no more.

V.

WHEN roses cease to bloom, dear,
  And violets are done,
When bumble-bees in solemn flight
  Have passed beyond the sun,

The hand that paused to gather
  Upon this summer's day
Will idle lie, in Auburn,–
  Then take my flower, pray!

VI.

SUMMER for thee grant I may be
  When summer days are flown!
Thy music still when whippoorwill
  And oriole are done!

For thee to bloom, I'll skip the tomb
  And sow my blossoms o'er!
Pray gather me, Anemone,
  Thy flower forevermore!

VII.

SPLIT the lark and you'll find the music,
    Bulb after bulb, in silver rolled,
Scantily dealt to the summer morning,
    Saved for your ear when lutes be old.

Loose the flood, you shall find it patent,
    Gush after gush, reserved for you;
Scarlet experiment! sceptic Thomas,
    Now, do you doubt that your bird was true?

VIII.

TO lose thee, sweeter than to gain
    All other hearts I knew.
'T is true the drought is destitute,
But then I had the dew!

The Caspian has its realms of sand,
    Its other realm of sea;
Without the sterile perquisite
    No Caspian could be.

IX.

POOR little heart!
             Did they forget thee?
Then dinna care! Then dinna care!

             Proud little heart!
Did they forsake thee?
Be debonair! Be debonair!

             Frail little heart!
I would not break thee:
Could'st credit me? Could'st credit me?

             Gay little heart!
Like morning glory
Thou'll wilted be; thou'll wilted be!

X.

THERE is a word
    Which bears a sword
  Can pierce an armed man.
It hurls its barbed syllables,–
  At once is mute again.
But where it fell
The saved will tell
  On patriotic day,
Some epauletted brother
  Gave his breath away.

Wherever runs the breathless sun,
  Wherever roams the day,
There is its noiseless onset,
  There is its victory!
Behold the keenest marksman!
  The most accomplished shot!
Time's sublimest target
Is a soul "forgot"!

XI.

I'VE got an arrow here;
    Loving the hand that sent it,
I the dart revere.

Fell, they will say in "skirmish"!
  Vanquished, my soul will know,
By but a simple arrow
  Sped by an archer's bow.

XII.

HE fumbles at your spirit
     As players at the keys
Before they drop full music on;
     He stuns you by degrees,

Prepares your brittle substance
     For the ethereal blow,
By fainter hammers, further heard,
     Then nearer, then so slow

Your breath has time to straighten,
     Your brain to bubble cool,–
Deals one imperial thunderbolt
     That scalps your naked soul.

XIII.

HEART, we will forget him!
     You and I, to-night!
You may forget the warmth he gave,
     I will forget the light.

When you have done, pray tell me,
     That I my thoughts may dim;
Haste! lest while you're lagging,
     I may remember him!

XIV.

FATHER, I bring thee not myself,–
        That were the little load;
I bring thee the imperial heart
    I had not strength to hold.

The heart I cherished in my own
        Till mine too heavy grew,
Yet strangest, heavier since it went,
    Is it too large for you?

XV.

WE outgrow love like other things
        And put it in the drawer,
Till it an antique fashion shows
    Like costumes grandsires wore.

XVI.

NOT with a club the heart is broken,
   Nor with a stone;
A whip, so small you could not see it.
  I've known

To lash the magic creature
  Till it fell,
Yet that whip's name too noble
  Then to tell.

Magnanimous of bird
  By boy descried,
To sing unto the stone
  Of which it died.

XVII.

MY friend must be a bird,
  Because it flies!
Mortal my friend must be,
  Because it dies!
Barbs has it, like a bee.
Ah, curious friend,
   Thou puzzlest me!

XVIII.

HE touched me, so I live to know
        That such a day, permitted so,
I groped upon his breast.
It was a boundless place to me,
And silenced, as the awful sea
        Puts minor streams to rest.

And now, I'm different from before,
As if I breathed superior air,
        Or brushed a royal gown;
My feet, too, that had wandered so,
My gypsy face transfigured now
        To tenderer renown.

XIX.

LET me not mar that perfect dream
        By an auroral stain,
But so adjust my daily night
        That it will come again.

XX.

I LIVE with him, I see his face;
        I go no more away
For visitor, or sundown;
        Death's single privacy,

The only one forestalling mine,
        And that by right that he
Presents a claim invisible,
        No wedlock granted me.

I live with him, I hear his voice,
        I stand alive to-day
To witness to the certainty
        Of immortality

Taught me by Time,—the lower way,
        Conviction every day,—
That life like this is endless,
        Be judgment what it may.

XXI.

I ENVY seas whereon he rides,
        I envy spokes of wheels
Of chariots that him convey,
        I envy speechless hills

That gaze upon his journey;
        How easy all can see
What is forbidden utterly
        As heaven, unto me!

I envy nests of sparrows
    That dot his distant eaves,
The wealthy fly upon his pane,
    The happy, happy leaves

That just abroad his window
    Have summer's leave to be,
The earrings of Pizarro
    Could not obtain for me.

I envy light that wakes him,
    And bells that boldly ring
To tell him it is noon abroad,–
    Myself his noon could bring,

Yet interdict my blossom
    And abrogate my bee,
Lest noon in everlasting night
    Drop Gabriel and me.

XXII.

A SOLEMN thing it was, I said,
    A woman white to be,
And wear, if God should count me fit,
    Her hallowed mystery.

A timid thing to drop a life
    Into the purple well,
Too plummetless that it come back
    Eternity until.

III. Nature

I.

THE springtime's pallid landscape
    Will glow like bright bouquet,
Through drifted deep in parian
    The village lies to-day.

The lilacs, bending many a year,
    With purple load will hang;
The bees will not forget the tune
    Their old forefathers sang.

The rose will redden in the bog,
    The aster on the hill
Her everlasting fashion set,
    And covenant gentians frill,

Till summer folds her miracle
    As women do their gown,
Or priests adjust the symbols
    When sacrament is done.

II.

SHE slept beneath a tree
    Remembered but by me.
I touched her cradle mute;
She recognized the foot,
Put on her carmine suit,—
    And see!

III.

A LIGHT exists in spring
    Not present on the year
At any other period.
    When March is scarcely here

A color stands abroad
    On solitary hills
That science cannot overtake,
    But human nature *feels*.

It waits upon the lawn;
    It shows the furthest tree
Upon the furthest slope we know;
    It almost speaks to me.

Then, as horizons step,
    Or noons report away,
Without the formula of sound.
    It passes, and we stay:

A quality of loss
    Affecting our content,
As trade had suddenly encroached
    Upon a sacrament.

IV.

A LADY red upon the hill
    Her annual secret keeps;
A lady white within the field
    In placid lily sleeps!

The tidy breezes with their brooms
    Sweep vale, and hill, and tree!
Prithee, my pretty housewives!
    Who may expected by?

The neighbors do not yet suspect!
    The woods exchange a smile—
Orchard, and buttercup, and bird—
    In such a little while!

And yet how still the landscape stands,
    How nonchalant the wood,
As if the resurrection
    Were nothing very odd!

V.

DEAR March, come in!
    How glad I am!
I looked for you before.
Put down your hat—
You must have walked—
How out of breath you are!
Dear March, how are you?
And the rest?
Did you leave Nature well?
Oh, March, come right upstairs with me,
I have so much to tell!

I got the letter, and the birds';
The maples never knew
That you were coming,—I declare,
How red their faces grew!
But, March, forgive me—
And all those hills
You left for me to hue;
There was no purple suitable,
You took it all with you.

Who knocks? That April!
Lock the door!
I will not be pursued!
He stayed away a year, to call
When I am occupied.
But trifles look so trivial
As soon as you have come,
That blame is just as dear as praise
And praise as mere as blame.

VI.

WE like March, his shoes are purple,
    He is new and high;
Makes he mud for dog and peddler,
    Makes he forest dry;
Knows the adder's tongue his coming,
    And begets her spot.
Stands the sun so close and mighty
    That our minds are hot.
News is he of all the others;
    Bold it were to die
With the blue-birds buccaneering
    On his British sky.

VII.

NOT knowing when the dawn will come
    I open every door;
Or has it feathers like a bird,
    Or billows like a shore?

VIII.

A MURMUR in the trees to note,
    Not loud enough for wind;
A star not far enough to seek,
    Nor near enough to find;

A long, long yellow on the lawn,
    A hubbub as of feet;
Not audible, as ours to us,
    But dapperer, more sweet;

A hurrying home of little men
    To houses unperceived,–
All this, and more, if I should tell,
    Would never be believed.

Of robins in the trundle bed
    How many I espy
Whose nightgowns could not hide the wings,
    Although I heard them try!

But then I promised ne'er to tell;
    How could I break my word?
So go your way and I'll go mine,–
    No fear you'll miss the road.

IX.

MORNING is the place for dew,
        Corn is made at noon,
After dinner light for flowers,
    Dukes for setting sun!

X.

TO my quick ear the leaves conferred;
        The bushes they were bells;
I could not find a privacy
    From Nature's sentinels.

In cave if I presumed to hide,
    The walls began to tell;
Creation seemed a mighty crack
    To make me visible.

XI.

A SEPAL, petal, and a thorn
        Upon a common summer's morn,
A flash of dew, a bee or two,
A breeze
A caper in the trees,—
    And I'm a rose!

XII.

HIGH from the earth I heard a bird;
　　He trod upon the trees
As he esteemed them trifles,
　　And then he spied a breeze,
And situated softly
　　Upon a pile of wind
Which in a perturbation
　　Nature had left behind.
A joyous-going fellow
　　I gathered from his talk,
Which both of benediction
　　And badinage partook,
Without apparent burden,
　　I learned, in leafy wood
He was the faithful father
　　Of a dependent brood;
And this untoward transport
　　His remedy of care,–
A contrast to our respites.
　　How different we are!

XIII.

THE spider as an artist
　　Has never been employed
Though his surpassing merit
　　Is freely certified

By every broom and Bridget
　　Throughout a Christian land.
Neglected son of genius,
　　I take thee by the hand.

XIV.

WHAT mystery pervades a well!
   The water lives so far,
Like neighbor from another world
   Residing in a jar.

The grass does not appear afraid;
   I often wonder he
Can stand so close and look so bold
   At what is dread to me.

Related somehow they may be,–
   The sedge stands next the sea,
Where he is floorless, yet of fear
   No evidence gives he.

But nature is stranger yet;
   The ones that cite her most
Have never passed her haunted house,
   Nor simplified her ghost.

To pity those that know her not
   Is helped by the regret
That those who know her, know her less
   The nearer her they get.

XV.

TO make a prairie it takes a clover
   and one bee,–
One clover, and a bee,
And revery.
The revery alone will do
If bees are few.

XVI.

I T'S like the light,–
         A fashionless delight
It's like the bee,–
      A dateless melody.

   It's like the woods,
      Private like breeze,
Phraseless, yet it stirs
      The proudest trees.

It's like the morning,–
      Best when it's done,–
The everlasting clocks
      Chime noon.

XVII.

A DEW sufficed itself
         And satisfied a leaf,
And felt, "how vast a destiny!
      How trivial is life!"

The sun went out to work,
      The day went out to play,
But not again that dew was seen
      By physiognomy.

Whether by day abducted,
      Or emptied by the sun
Into the sea, in passing,
      Eternally unknown.

XVIII.

HIS bill an auger is,
      His head, a cap and frill.
He laboreth at every tree,–
   A worm his utmost goal.

XIX.

SWEET is the swamp with its secrets,
      Until we meet a snake;
'T is then we sigh for houses,
   And our departure take
At that enthralling gallop
   That only childhood knows.
A snake is summer's treason,
   And guile is where it goes.

XX.

COULD I but ride indefinite,
        As doth the meadow-bee,
And visit only where I liked,
        And no man visit me,

And flirt all day with buttercups,
        And marry whom I may,
And dwell a little everywhere,
        Or better, run away

With no police to follow,
        Or chase me if I do,
Till I should jump peninsulas
        To get away from you,–

I said, but just to be a bee
        Upon a raft of air,
And row in nowhere all day
long,
        And anchor off the bar,–
What liberty! So captives deem
        Who tight in dungeons are.

XXI.

THE moon was but a chin of gold
    A night or two ago,
And now she turns her perfect face
    Upon the world below.

Her forehead is of amplest blond;
    Her cheek like beryl stone;
Her eye unto the summer dew
    The likest I have known.

Her lips of amber never part;
    But what must be the smile
Upon her friend she could bestow
    Were such her silver will!

And what a privilege to be
    But the remotest star!
For certainly her way might pass
    Beside your twinkling door.

Her bonnet is the firmament,
    The universe her shoe,
The stars the trinkets at her belt,
    Her dimities of blue.

XXII.

THE bat is dun with wrinkled wings
     Like fallow article,
And not a song pervades his lips,
     Or none perceptible.

His small umbrella, quaintly halved,
     Describing in the air
An arc alike inscrutable,—
     Elate philosopher!

Deputed from what firmament
     Of what astute abode,
Empowered with what malevolence
     Auspiciously withheld.

To his adroit Creator
     Ascribe no less the praise;
Beneficent, believe me,
     His eccentricities.

XXIII.

YOU'VE seen balloons set, have n't you?
      So stately they ascend
It is as swans discarded you
      For duties diamond.

Their liquid feet go softly out
      Upon a sea of blond;
They spurn the air as 't were too mean
      For creatures so renowned.

Their ribbons just beyond the eye,
      They struggle some for breath,
And yet the crowd applauds below;
      They would not encore death.

The gilded creature strains and spins,
      Trips frantic in a tree,
Tears open her imperial veins
      And tumbles in the sea.

The crowd retire with an oath
      The dust in streets goes down,
And clerks in counting-rooms observe,
      "'T was only a balloon."

XXIV.

THE cricket sang,
        And set the sun,
And workmen finished, one by one,
    Their seam the day upon.

The low grass loaded with the dew,
The twilight stood as strangers do
With hat in hand, polite and new,
    To stay as if, or go.

A vastness, as a neighbor, came,–
A wisdom without face or name,
A peace, as hemispheres at home,–
    And so the night became.

XXV.

DRAB habitation of whom?
        Tabernacle or tomb,
Or dome of worm,
Or porch of gnome,
Or some elf's catacomb?

XXVI.

A SLOOP of amber slips away
        Upon an ether sea,
And wrecks in peace a purple tar,
    The son of ecstasy.

XXVII.

OF bronze and blaze
    The north, to-night!
So adequate its forms,
So preconcerted with itself,
    So distant to alarms,–
An unconcern so sovereign
    To universe, or me,
It paints my simple spirit
    With tints of majesty,
Till I take vaster attitudes,
    And strut upon my stem,
Disdaining men and oxygen,
    For arrogance of them.

My splendors are menagerie;
    But their competeless show
Will entertain the centuries
    When I am, long ago,
An island in dishonored grass,
    Whom none but daisies know.

XXVIII.

HOW the old mountains drip with sunset,
    And the brake of dun!
How the hemlocks are tipped in tinsel
    By the wizard sun!

How the old steeples hand the scarlet,
    Till the ball is full,–
Have I the lip of the flamingo
    That I dare to tell?

Then, how the fire ebbs like billows,
  Touching all the grass
With a departing, sapphire feature,
  As if a duchess pass!

How a small dusk crawls on the village
  Till the houses blot;
And the odd flambeaux no men carry
  Glimmer on the spot!
Now it is night in nest and kennel,
  And where was the wood,
Just a dome of abyss is nodding
  Into solitude! –

These are the visions baffled Guido;
  Titian never told;
Domenichino dropped the pencil,
  Powerless to unfold.

XXIX.

THE murmuring of bees has ceased;
  But murmuring of some
Posterior, prophetic,
  Has simultaneous come,–

The lower metres of the year,
  When nature's laugh is done,–
The Revelations of the book
  Whose Genesis is June.

IV. Time and Eternity

I.

THIS world is not conclusion;
    A sequel stands beyond,
Invisible, as music,
    But positive, as sound.
It beckons and it baffles;
    Philosophies don't know,
And through a riddle, at the last,
    Sagacity must go.
To guess it puzzles scholars;
To gain it, men have shown
Contempt of generations,
    And crucifixion known.

II.

WE learn in the retreating
    How vast an one
Was recently among us.
    A perished sun

Endears in the departure
    How doubly more
Than all the golden presence
    It was before!

III.

THEY say that "time assuages,"–
        Time never did assuage;
An actual suffering strengthens,
        As sinews do, with age.

Time is a test of trouble,
        But not a remedy.
If such it prove, it prove too
        There was no malady.

IV.

WE cover thee, sweet face.
        Not that we tire of thee,
But that thyself fatigue of us;
        Remember, as thou flee,
We follow thee until
        Thou notice us no more,
And then, reluctant, turn away
        To con thee o'er and o'er,
Ad blame the scanty love
        We were content to show,
Augmented, sweet, a hundred fold
        If thou would'st take it now.

V.

THAT is solemn we have ended, –
    Be it but a play,
Or a glee among the garrets,
    Or a holiday,

Or a leaving home; or later,
    Parting with a world
We have understood, for better
    Still it be unfurled.

VI.

THE stimulus, beyond the grave
    His countenance to see,
Supports me like imperial drams
    Afforded royally.

VII.

GIVEN in marriage unto thee,
    Oh, thou celestial host!
Bride of the Father and the Son,
    Bride of the Holy Ghost!

Other betrothal shall dissolve,
    Wedlock of will decay;
Only the keeper of this seal
    Conquers mortality.

VIII.

THAT such have died enables us
　　The tranquiller to die;
That such have lived, certificate
　　For immortality.

IX.

THEY won't frown always,—some sweet day
　　When I forget to tease,
They'll recollect how cold I looked,
　　And how I just said "please."

Then they will hasten to the door
　　To call the little child,
Who cannot thank them, for the ice
　　That on her lisping piled.

X.

IT is an honorable thought,
　　And makes one lift one's hat,
As one encountered gentlefolk
　　Upon a daily street,

That we've immortal place,
　　Though pyramids decay,
And kingdoms, like the orchard,
　　Flit russetly away.

XI.

THE distance that the dead have gone
        Does not at first appear;
Their coming back seems possible
    For many an ardent year.

And then, that we have followed them
    We more than half suspect,
So intimate have we become
    With their dear retrospect.

XII.

HOW dare the robins sing,
        When men and women hear
Who since they went to their account
    Have settled with the year! —
Paid all that life had earned
    In one consummate bill,
And now, what life or death can do
    Is immaterial.
Insulting is the sun
    To him whose mortal light,
Beguiled of immortality,
    Bequeaths him to the night.
In deference to him
    Extinct be every hum,
Whose garden wrestles with the dew,
    At daybreak overcome!

XIII.

DEATH is like the insect
        Menacing the tree,
Competent to kill it,
        But decoyed may be.

Bait it with the balsam,
        Seek it with the knife,
Baffle, if it cost you
        Everything in life.

Then, if it have burrowed
        Out of reach of skill,
Ring the tree and leave it, —
        'T is the vermin's will.

XIV.

'T IS sunrise, little maid, hast thou
    No station in the day?
'T was not thy wont to hinder so,–
    Retrieve thine industry.

'T is noon, my little maid, alas!
    And art thou sleeping yet?
The lily waiting to be wed,
    The bee, dost thou forget?

My little maid, 't is night; alas,
    That night should be to thee
Instead of morning! Hadst thou broached
    Thy little plan to me,
Dissuade thee if I could not, sweet,
    I might have aided thee.

XV.

EACH that we lose takes part of us;
    A crescent still abides,
Which like the moon, some turbid night,
    Is summoned by the tides.

XVI.

NOT any higher stands the grave
    For heroes than for men;
Not any nearer for the child
    Than numb three-score and ten.

This latest leisure equal lulls
    The beggar and his queen;
Propitiate this democrat
    By summer's gracious mien.

XVII.

AS far from pity as complaint,
    As cool to speech as stone,
As numb to revelation
    As if my trade were bone.

As far from time as history,
    As near yourself to-day
As children to the rainbow's scarf,
    Or sunset's yellow play

To eyelids in the sepulchre.
    How still the dancer lies,
While color's revelations break,
    And blaze the butterflies!

XVIII.

'T IS whiter than an Indian pipe;
    'T is dimmer than a lace;
No stature has it, like a fog,
    When you approach the place.

Not any voice denotes it here,
    Or intimates it there;
A spirit, how doth it accost?
    What customs hath the air?

This limitless hyperbole
    Each one of us shall be;
'T is drama, if (hypothesis)
    It be not tragedy!

XIX.

SHE laid her docile crescent down,
    And this mechanic stone
Still states, to dates that have forgot,
    The news that she is gone.

So constant to its stolid trust,
    The shaft that never knew,
It shames the constancy that fled
    Before its emblem flew.

XX.

BLESS God, he went as soldiers,
    His musket on his breast;
Grant, God, he charge the bravest
    Of all the martial blest.

Please God, might I behold him
    In ipauletted white,
I should not fear the foe then,
    I should not fear the fight.

XXI.

IMMORTAL is an ample word
    When what we need is by,
But when it leaves us for a time,
    'T is a necessity.

Of heaven above the firmest proof
    We fundamental know,
Except for its marauding hand,
    It had been heaven below.

XXII.

WHERE every bird is bold to go,
    And bees abashless play,
The foreigner before he knocks
    Must thrust the tears away.

XXIII.

THE grave my little cottage is,
    Where, keeping house for thee,
I make my parlor orderly,
    And lay the marble tea,

For two divided, briefly,
    A cycle, it may be,
Till everlasting life unite
    In strong society.

XXIV.

THIS was in the white of the year,
    That was in the green,
Drifts were as difficult then to think
    As daisies now to be seen.

Looking back is best that is left,
    Or if it be before,
Retrospection is prospect's half,
    Sometimes almost more.

XXV.

SWEET hours have perished here;
    This is a mighty room;
Within its precincts hopes have played,—
    Now shadows in the tomb.

XXVI.

ME! Come! My dazzled face
          In such a shining place!

Me! Hear! My foreign ear
The sounds of welcome near!

The saints shall meet
Our bashful feet.

My holiday shall be
That they remember me;

My paradise, the fame
That they pronounce my name.

XXVII.

FROM us she wandered now a year,
          Her tarrying unknown;
If wilderness prevent her feet,
          Or that ethereal zone

No eye hath seen and lived,
          We ignorant must be.
We only know what time of year
          We took the mystery.

XXVIII.

I WISH I knew that woman's name,
    So, when she comes this way,
To hold my life, and hold my ears,
    For fear I hear her say

She's "sorry I am dead," again,
    Just when the grave and I
Have sobbed ourselves almost to sleep, –
    Our only lullaby.

XXIX.

BEREAVED of all, I went abroad,
    No less bereaved to be
Upon a new peninsula, –
    The grave preceded me,

Obtained my lodgings ere myself,
    And when I sought my bed,
The grave it was, reposed upon
    The pillow for my head.

I waked, to find it first awake,
    I rose, – it followed me;
I tried to drop it in the crowd,
    To lose it in the sea,

In cups of artificial drowse
    To sleep its shape away, –
The grave finished, but the spade
    Remained in memory.

XXX.

I FELT a funeral in my brain,
    And mourners, to and fro,
Kept treading, treading, till it seemed
    That sense was breaking through.

And when they all were seated,
    A service like a drum
Kept beating, beating, till I thought
    My mind was going numb.

And then I heard them lift a box,
    And creak across my soul
With those same boots of lead, again.
    Then space began to toll

As all the heavens were a bell,
    And Being but an ear,
And I and silence some strange race,
    Wrecked, solitary, here.

XXXI.

I MEANT to find her when I came;
    Death had the same design;
But the success was his, it seems,
    And the discomfit mine.

I meant to tell her how I longed
    For just this single time;
But Death had told her so the first,
    And she had harkened him.

To wander now is my abode;
   To rest,–to rest would be
A privilege of hurricane
   To memory and me.

XXXII.

I SING to use the waiting,
   My bonnet but to tie,
And shut the door unto my house;
   No more to do have I,

Till, his best step approaching,
   We journey to the day,
And tell each other how we sang
   To keep the dark away.

XXXIII.

A SICKNESS of this world it most occasions
   When best men die;
A wishfulness their far condition
   To occupy.

A chief indifference, as foreign
   A world must be
Themselves forsake contented,
   For Deity.

XXXIV.

SUPERFLUOUS were the sun
        When excellence is dead;
He were superfluous every day,
    For every day is said

That syllable whose faith
    Just saves it from despair,
And whose "I'll meet you" hesitates
    If love inquire, "Where?"

Upon his dateless fame
    Our periods may lie,
As stars that drop anonymous
    From an abundant sky.

XXXV.

SO proud she was to die
        It made us all ashamed
That what we cherished, so unknown
    To her desire seemed.

So satisfied to go
    Where none of us should be,
Immediately, that anguish stooped
    Almost to jealousy.

XXXVI.

TIE the strings to my life, my Lord,
    Then I am ready to go!
Just a look at the horses –
    Rapid! That will do!

Put me in on the firmest side,
    So I shall never fall;
For we must ride to the Judgment,
    And it's partly down hill.

But never I mind the bridges,
    And never I mind the sea;
Held fast in everlasting race
    By my own choice and thee.

Good-by to the life I used to live,
    And the world I used to know;
And kiss the hills for me, just once;
    Now I am ready to go!

XXXVII.

THE dying need but little, dear, –
    A glass of water's all,
A flower's unobtrusive face
    To punctuate the wall,

A fan, perhaps, a friend's regret,
    And certainly that one
No color in the rainbow
    Perceives when you are gone.

XXXVIII.

THERE'S something quieter than sleep
        Within this inner room!
It wears a sprig upon its breast,
        And will not tell its name.

Some touch it and some kiss it,
        Some chafe its idle hand;
It has a simple gravity
        I do not understand!

While simple-hearted neighbors
        Chat of the "early dead,"
We, prone to periphrasis,
        Remark that birds have fled!

XXXIX.

THE soul should always stand ajar,
        That if the heaven inquire,
He will not be obliged to wait,
        Or shy of troubling her.

Depart, before the host has slid
        The bolt upon the door,
To seek for the accomplished guest,–
        Her visitor no more.

XL.

THREE weeks passed since I had seen her, –
    Some disease had vexed;
'T was with text and village singing
    I beheld her next,
And a company – our pleasure
    To discourse alone;
Gracious now to me as any,
    Gracious unto none.

Borne, without dissent of either,
    To the parish night;
Of the separated people
    Which are out of sight?

XLI.

I BREATHED enough to learn the trick,
    And now, removed from air,
I simulate the breath so well,
    That one, to be quite sure

The lungs are stirless, must descend
    Among the cunning cells,
And touch the pantomine himself.
    How cool the bellows feels!

XLII.

I WONDER if the sepulchre
        Is not a lonesome way,
When men and boys, and larks and June
    Go down the fields to hay!

XLIII.

IF tolling bell I ask the cause.
        "A soul has gone to God,"
I'm answered in a lonesome tone;
    Is heaven then so sad?

That bells should joyful ring to tell
    A soul had gone to heaven,
Would seem to me the proper way
    A good news should be given.

XLIV.

IF I may have it when it's dead
    I will contented be;
If just as soon as breath is out
It shall belong to me,

Until they lock it in the grave,
    'T is bliss I cannot weigh,
For though they lock thee in the grave,
    Myself can hold the key.

Think of it, lover! I and thee
    Permitted face to face to be;
After a life, a death we'll say,–
    For death was that, and this is thee.

XLV.

BEFORE the ice is in the pools,
    Before the skaters go,
Or any cheek at nightfall
    Is tarnished by the snow,

Before the fields have finished,
    Before the Christmas tree,
Wonder upon wonder
    Will arrive to me!

What we touch the hems of
    On a summer's day;
What is only walking
    Just a bridge away;

That which sings so, speaks so,
    When there's no one here,–
Will the frock I wept in
    Answer me to wear?

XLVI.

I HEARD a fly buzz when I died;
    The stillness round my form
Was like the stillness in the air
    Between the heaves of storm.

The eyes beside had wrung them dry,
    And breaths were gathering sure
For that last onset, when the king
    Be witnessed in his power.

I willed my keepsakes, signed away
    What portion of me I
Could make assignable,–and then
    There interposed a fly,

With blue, uncertain, stumbling buzz,
    Between the light and me;
And then the windows failed, and then
    I could not see to see.

XLVII.

ADRIFT! A little boat adrift!
    And night is coming down!
Will no one guide a little boat
    Unto the nearest town?

So sailors say, on yesterday,
    Just as the dusk was brown,
One little boat gave up its strife,
    And gurgled down and down.

But angels say, on yesterday,
    Just as the dawn was red,
One little boat gave up its strife,
    And gurgled down and down.

But angels say, on yesterday,
    Just as the dawn was red,
One little boat o'erspent with gales
Retrimmed its masts, redecked its sails
    Exultant, onward sped!

XLVIII.

THERE'S been a death in the opposite house
        As lately as to-day.
I know it by the numb look
        Such houses have alway.

The neighbors rustle in and out,
        The doctor drives away.
A window opens like a pod,
        Abrupt, mechanically;

Somebody flings a mattress out,–
        The children hurry by;
They wonder if It died on that,–
        I used to when a boy.

The minister goes stiffly in
        As if the house were his,
And he owned all the mourners now,
        And little boys besides;

And then the milliner, and the man
        Of the appalling trade,
To take the measure of the house.
        There'll be that dark parade

Of tassels and of coaches soon;
        It's easy as a sign,–
The intuition of the news
        In just a country town.

XLIX.

WE never know we go,–when we are going
        We jest and shut the door;
Fate following behind us bolts it,
        And we accost no more.

L.

IT struck me every day
        The lightning was as new
As if the cloud that instant slit
        And let the fire through.

It burned me in the night,
        It blistered in my dream;
It sickened fresh upon my sight
        With every morning's beam.

I thought that storm was brief,–
        The maddest, quickest by;
But Nature lost the date of this,
        And left it in the sky.

LI.

WATER is taught by thirst;
     Land, by the oceans passed;
Transport, by throe;
Peace, by its battles told;
Love, by memorial mould;
     Birds, by the snow.

LII.

WE thirst at first,—'t is Nature's act;
     And later, when we die,
A little water supplicate
     Of fingers going by.

It intimates the finer want,
     Whose adequate supply
Is that great water in the west
     Termed immortality.

LIII.

A CLOCK stopped—not the mantel's;
    Geneva's farthest skill
Can't put the puppet bowing
    That just now dangled still.

An awe came on the trinket!
    The figures hunched with pain,
Then quivered out of decimals
    Into degreeless noon.

It will not stir for doctors,
    This pendulum of snow;
The shopman importunes it,
    While cool, concernless No

Nods from the gilded pointers,
    Nods from the seconds slim,
Decades of arrogance between
    The dial life and him.

LIV.

ALL overgrown by cunning moss,
      All interspersed with weed,
The little cage of "Currer Bell,"
      In quiet Haworth laid.

This bird, observing others,
      When frosts too sharp became,
Retire to other latitudes,
      Quietly did the same,

But differed in returning;
      Since Yorkshire hills are green,
Yet not in all the nests I meet
      Can nightingale be seen.

Gathered from many wanderings,
      Gethsemane can tell
Through what transporting anguish
      She reached the asphodel!

Soft fall the sounds of Eden
      Upon her puzzled ear;
Oh, what an afternoon for heaven,
      When "Brontë" entered there!

LV.

A TOAD can die of light!
     Death is the common right
Of toads and men,–
Of earl and midge
The privilege.
     Why swagger then?
The gnat's supremacy
Is large as thine.

LVI.

FAR from love the Heavenly Father
     Leads the chosen child;
Oftener through realm of briar
     Than the meadow mild,

Oftener by the claw of dragon
     Than the hand of friend,
Guides the little one predestined
     To the native land.

LVII.

A LONG, long sleep, a famous sleep
    That makes no show for dawn
By stretch of limb or stir of lid,—
    An independent one.

Was ever idleness like this?
    Within a hut of stone
To bask the centuries away
    Nor once look up for noon?

LVIII.

'T WAS just this time last year I died.
    I know I heard the corn,
When I was carried by the farms,—
    It had tassels on.

I thought how yellow it would look
    When Richard went to mill;
And then I wanted to get out,
    But something held my will.

I thought just how red apples wedged
    The stubble's joints between;
And carts went stooping round the fields
    To take the pumpkins in.

I wondered which would miss me least,
    And then Thanksgiving came
As father'd multiply the plates
    To make an even sum.

And if my stocking hung too high,
    Would it blur the Christmas glee,
That not a Santa Claus could reach
    The altitude of me?

But this sort grieved myself, and so
    I thought how it would be
When just this time, some perfect year,
    Themselves should come to me.

LIX.

ON this wondrous sea,
        Sailing silently,
Ho! pilot, ho!
Knowest thou the shore
Where no breakers roar,
        Where the storm is o'er?

In the silent west
Many sails at rest,
        Their anchors fast;
Thither I pilot thee,—
Land, ho! Eternity!
        Ashore at last!

· · ·

THE SINGLE HOUND

POEMS OF A LIFETIME

BY

EMILY DICKINSON

. . .

PREFACE

THE romantic friendship of my Aunt Emily Dickinson and her
"Sister Sue" extended from girlhood until death. The
first poem, dated, was sent in 1848, and probably the last word
Aunt Emily ever wrote was her reply to a message from my
Mother, "My answer is an unmitigated Yes, Sue." During the last
year of my Mother's life she read and re-read these poems, and
innumerable letters, with increasing indecision as to the final
disposition of her treasury. It eventually devolved upon me to
choose between burning them or giving them to the lovers of
my Aunt's peculiar genius.

My hesitation was finally influenced by a note written in
their early twenties, which I quote.

DEAR SUE:

I like your praise because I know it knows. If I could make
you and Austin proud some day a long way off, 'twould give me
taller feet.

EMILY.

This is my inspiration for a volume, offered as a memorial to
the love of these "Dear, dead Women."

Also, it seemed but fitting to reveal a phase of Aunt Emily
known only to us who dwelt with her behind the hedge; the
fascinating, wilful woman, lightning and fragrance in one.

I am told she is taught in colleges as a rare strange being; a
weird recluse, eating her heart out in morbid and unhappy
longing, or a victim of unsatisfied passion; I have heard her
called "an epigrammatic Walt Whitman" by a noted lecturer,

and only recently a distinguished foreign critic pronounced her "the greatest mystic America has produced – second only to Ralph Waldo Emerson."

But to her niece and nephews she was of fairy lineage, akin to the frost on the nursery pane in Winter or the humming bird or Midsummer; the realization of our vivid fancy, the confederate in every contraband desire, the very Spirit of the "Never, Never Land."

She adored us, her three Child-Lovers, talked to us as if we were grown up and our opinions of importance, our secrets portentous, though always keeping herself our playmate with such art that she remains in my memory as a little girl herself. Once, when my brother Ned, as a child, stood looking up at the evening star, he said wistfully, "I want to go up there, Aunt Emily." "All right," she cried, "Go get your horse and buggy and we'll go tonight!" Often quoting afterward his grave rebuke of her levity – "Aunt Emily, – you can't go up there in a horse and buggy!"

When we were happy she added her crumb, when we were ill all she had was ours, were we grieved, her indignation was hot against whoever or whatever had wounded us. I thought of her as the avenging angel then, her eyes smouldered so gloriously at our wrongs. One other charm was unique to her; her way of flitting, like a shadow upon the hillside, a motion known to no other mortal. In the midst of one of our Eden-hours, she would fly at the sound of an intruder and was not – only the tick of the old clock left for our companioning. I was usually left with her while both families went to church on Sabbath mornings and well remember being escorted by her down to the cool hoarding cellar, past the wine closet to a mysterious cupboard of her own, where she dealt me such lawless cake and other goodies, that even a child of four knew it for excess, sure to be followed by disaster later in the day. There was an unreal abandon about it all such as thrills the prodigality of dreaming.

As we grew older her wit was our unconscious standard of others, her pitiless directness of thought our revelation, while her sweetness was like nothing but that of her own favorite jasmine flowers. Indeed she resembled the Cape Jasmine more than any mortal being. They two were the whitest Sisters, or flowers, Nature ever bore.

Once let us get to her – past what Mr. Henry James calls "an archaic Irish servant," past our other faithful but prejudiced Aunt Lavinia, who gave us a plain cookey and advised us to "run home,"– once within the forbidden precincts of the "front part" of the old mansion, we had found our South-West passage and were transported, obstinate, oblivious. To water her plants with her tiny watering pot, to help her ice a loaf of plum cake for her Father's supper, to watch her check off the rich dark caramels she unfailingly kept on hand for us, to share her wickedness in skirmishing to avoid outsiders, or to connive in her intrigue to outwit the cat of perpetual unpopularity in her esteem,– what other joys could drag us from these?

She put more excitement into the event of a dead fly than her neighbors got from a journey by stage-coach to Boston. If art is *"exaggeration apropos,"* as Mérimée claims, she was an incomparable artist at life.

There was nothing forbidden us by her, in spite of which license we were as shy of troubling her, as gentle in our play with her, as if she had been Hans Anderson's little Snow Maiden and might melt before our eyes if misunderstood.

Fascination was her element. It was my brother Ned, borne home against his will, screaming "I want a rich! I *will see* my Aunt Emily! I will have a rich!" who provided that dear Villain with a synonym for her own terms with Life. "A rich" was the desire of her heart, "a rich" was her instinctive claim, and she would not compromise.

The poems here included were written on any chance slip of paper, sometimes the old plaid Quadrille, sometimes a gilt-edged sheet with a Paris mark, often a random scrap of commercial note from her Father's law office. Each of these is folded over, addressed merely "Sue," and sent by the first available hand. For though they lived side by side with only a wide green lawn between, days and even weeks slipped by sometimes without their actual meeting. My Mother was blessedly busy in her home and Aunt Emily's light across the snow in the Winter gloaming, or burning late when she remained up all night, to protect her plants from chill, was often a mute greeting between them supplemented only by their written messages. There must have been a lure for the almost cloistered soul in the warmth of her only brother Austin's youthful home, and the radiant atmosphere of my Mother with her three children growing up about her. "Only Woman in the World," "Avalanche of Sun," "Sister of Ophir," she calls her. In these earlier days Aunt Emily often came over, most frequently in the evening, and always when Mr. Bowles, Mrs. Anthon of London, or some such cherished guest, was here. She played brilliantly upon the piano, and travestied the descriptive pieces popular at that period with as much skill as wit. One improvisation which she called *the Devil* was, by tradition, unparalleled. She had no idea of the passing of time when at the height of these frolics and not until my revered Grandfather appeared with his lantern, would the revel break off. Him she adored, feared, made fun of, and obeyed. "If Father is asleep on the sofa the house is full, though it were empty otherwise!" was one of her familiar exclamations. It could never be said of her, as she said of a prosaic friend, "He has the facts but not the phosphorescence of learning!" One evening when Dr. and Mrs. Holland had arrived unexpectedly to pass the night, having driven over from Northhampton in the Autumn dusk, my Grandmother, anxious for their every comfort, offered one solicitous suggestion after another, until Aunt Emily, always exasperated by repetition, cried –"O Mrs. Holland, don't you want to hear me say the Lord's prayer? Shouldn't you like me to repeat the Declaration of Independence? Shan't I recite the Ten Commandments?"

It was in this mood that she once put four superfluous kittens on the fire-shovel and softly dropped them into the first convenient jar the cellar offered, her family being in church – her chosen time for iniquity. This especial jar happened to be full of pickle brine. The sequel was very awful; occurring when the austere Judge Otis P. Lord of Salem was visiting my Grandfather, and as in all such emergencies of detection she fled to her own room and turned the key; holding reproach at bay until she chose to come out and ignore it. In her innocent love of mystery and intrigue Aunt Emily reminds one of Stevenson. She would have played at "lantern bearers" with him, and given the stealthy countersign under her breath, as no other living urchin!

She was "eternally preoccupied with death" as any of Pater's giant Florentines, but though the supernatural had the supreme hold on her imagination and conjecture, every lesser mystery was a panic and an ecstasy. If she could contrive to outwit domestic vigilance and smuggle a box of fresh-laid eggs to my Mother, on the sly, it savored to her of piracy and brigandage. She was averse to surveillance of every description and took pains to elude it in these little traffics of her heart as in the enigmas of her Being. "Give me liberty or give me death – but if you can, give me liberty!" was her frequent cry. She had a keen scent for the meanings hid beneath the goodly outside of diplomacy and watched for developments in home and foreign policies with surprising acumen. The Winter she was at Willard's, during her Father's Congressional career, she is said to have astonished his political friends by her insight and created quite a sensation by her wit, though the only story I recall now was of her saying to a prim old Chief Justice of the Supremest sort, when the plum pudding on fire was offered –

"Oh Sir, may one eat of hell fire with impunity, here?"

Physically timid at the least approach to a crisis in the day's event, her *mind* dared earth and heaven. That apocrypha and apocalypse met in her, explains her tendency so often mistaken for blasphemy by the superficial analyst.

The advance and retreat of her thought, her transition from arch to demure, from elfin to angelic, from soaring to drowning, her inescapable sense of tragedy, her inimitable perception of comedy, her breathless reverence and unabashed invasion upon the intimate affairs of Deity and hearsay of the Bible, made her a comrade to mettle inspiration and dazzle rivalry. Unlike the dullard, brilliancy was no effort for her. She revelled in the wings of her mind,—I had almost said the fins too,—so universal was her identification with every form of life and element of being. She usually liked men better than women because they were more stimulating. I can see her yet, standing in the spacious upper hall a Summer afternoon, finger on lip, and hear her say, as the feminine callers took their departure—"Listen! Hear them kiss, the traitors!" To most women she was a provoking puzzle. To her, in turn, most women were a form of triviality to be escaped when feasible.

But stupidity had no sex with her and I equally well remember her spying down upon a stranger sent to call upon her by a mutual friend, and dismissing him unreceived after one glance from her window, remarking—"His face is as handsome and as meaningless as the full moon." At another time she called me to peep at a new Professor recently come to the college, saying—"Look dear, he is pretty as a cloth Pink!" her mouth curling in derision as she uttered it and one hand motioning as if to throw the flower away. She had a dramatic way of throwing up her hands at the climax of a story or to punctuate one of her own flashes. It was entirely spontaneous, her spirit seemed merely playing through her body as the Aurora borealis through darkness. And since there is no portrait

of Aunt Emily, may I be pardoned if I try to give an idea of her
external likeness? It has been often told that she wore white
exclusively. She has said herself, in one of her letters to an
inquisitive friend who had never seen her and importuned for a
hint of her outward self,—that her eyes were the color of the
sherry left in the glass by him to whom she wrote. Her hair was
of that same warm bronze-chestnut hue that Titian immortalized,
and she wore it parted on her brow and low in her neck, but
always half covered by a velvet snood of the same tint; such as
the Venetian painters loved to add as a final grace to the
portraits of their beloved and beautiful women. Her cheek was
like the petal of the jasmine, a velvety white never touched by a
hint of color. Her red lips parted over very regular little teeth like
the squirrels' and it was the rather long upper lip that gave to the
mouth its asceticism, and betrayed the monastic tendency in her,
of which she was probably quite unaware.

If this combines nature and art and mysticism in one, too
bewilderingly to reproduce any definite impression, it is the
fault of that face,—as intimate in my memory as it is still in my
dreams.

In spite of an innate austerity of the senses, my Aunt had
lovers, like Browning's roses—"all the way"—to the end; men of
varied profession and attainment who wrote to her and came to
see her, and whose letters she burned with a chivalry not all of
them requited in kind. "Sister Sue" was her confidante and ally,
from whose lips we heard many a hot or quaint tale when time
had made them no perfidy. One of these in which we most
delighted was of how Aunt Emily as a young lady, having been
decorously driven to a funeral in Hadley, in the family barouche
lined with cream-colored broadcloth, ran from the grave with a
dashing cousin from Worcester, via a skittish black horse and
worldly buggy, capping her infamy by returning through
Sunderland and being in her room with the door locked when
the family got home.

Nothing would be more delicious to me than to repeat by name the list of those whom she bewitched. It included college boys, tutors, law students, the brothers of her girl friends,— several times their affianced bridegrooms even; and then the maturer friendships,—literary, Platonic, Plutonic; passages varying in intensity, and at least one passionate attachment whose tragedy was due to the integrity of the Lovers, who scrupled to take their bliss at another's cost.

She was not daily-bread. She was star-dust. Her solitude made her and was part of her. Taken from her distant sky she must have become a creature as different as fallen meteor from pulsing star. One may ask of the Sphinx, if life would not have been dearer to her, lived as other women lived it? To have been, in essence, more as other women were? Or if, in so doing and so being, she would have missed that inordinate compulsion, that inquisitive comprehension that made her Emily Dickinson? It is to ask again the old riddle of genius against every-day happiness. Had life or love been able to dissuade her from that "eternal preoccupation with death" which thralled her—if she could have chosen—you urge, still unconvinced? But I feel that she could and did, and that nothing could have compensated her for the forfeit of that "single hound," her "own Identity."

MARTHA DICKINSON BIANCHI.

. . .

PRELUDE

One Sister have I in our house,
And one a hedge away
There's only one recorded
But both belong to me.

One came the way that I came,
And wore my last year's gown,
The other, as a bird her nest,
Builded our hearts among.

She did not sing as we did,
It was a different tune,
Herself to her a music –
As Bumble-bee of June.

Today is far from childhood,
But up and down the hills
I held her hand the tighter,
Which shortened all the miles.

And still her hum the years among
Deceives the Butterfly,
Still in her eye the Violets lie
Mouldered this many May.

I split the dew but took the morn,
I chose this single Star
From out the wide night's numbers,
Sue—forevermore!

—Emilie.

I.

ADVENTURE most unto itself
  The Soul condemned to be;
Attended by a Single Hound –
Its own Identity.

II.

THE Soul that hath a Guest,
  Doth seldom go abroad,
Diviner Crowd at home
Obliterate the need,
And courtesy forbid
A Host's departure, when
Upon Himself be visiting
The Emperor of Men!

III.

EXCEPT the smaller size, no Lives are round,
  These hurry to a sphere, and show, and end.
The larger, slower grow, and later hang –
The Summers of Hesperides are long.

IV.

FAME is a fickle food
          Upon a shifting plate,
Whose table once a Guest, but not
The second time, is set.
Whose crumbs the crows inspect,
And with ironic caw
Flap past it to the Farmer's corn;
Men eat of it and die.

V.

THE right to perish might be thought
          An undisputed right,
Attempt it, and the Universe upon the opposite
Will concentrate its officers —
You cannot even die,
But Nature and Mankind must pause
To pay you scrutiny.

VI.

PERIL as a possession
          'T is good to bear,
Danger disintegrates satiety;
There's Basis there
Begets an awe,
That searches Human Nature's creases
As clean as Fire.

VII.

WHEN Etna basks and purrs,
        Naples is more afraid
Than when she shows her Garnet Tooth;
Security is loud.

VIII.

REVERSE cannot befall that fine Prosperity
        Whose sources are interior.
As soon Adversity
A diamond overtake,
In far Bolivian ground;
Misfortune hath no implement
Could mar it, if it found.

IX.

TO be alive is power,
        Existence in itself,
Without a further function,
Omnipotence enough.

To be alive and Will—
'T is able as a God!
The further of ourselves be what—
Such being Finitude?

X.

WITCHCRAFT has not a pedigree,
        'T is early as our breath,
And mourners meet it going out
The moment of our death.

XI.

EXHILARATION is the Breeze
        That lifts us from the ground,
And leaves us in another place
Whose statement is not found;
Returns us not, but after time
We soberly descend,
A little newer for the term
Upon enchanted ground.

XII.

NO romance sold unto,
        Could so enthrall a man
As the perusal of
His individual one.
'T is fiction's, to dilute
To plausibility
Our novel, when 't is small enough
To credit,—'t is n't true!

XIII

IF what we could were what we would –
      Criterion be small;
It is the Ultimate of talk
The impotence to tell.

XIV.

PERCEPTION of an
      Object costs
Precise the Object's loss.
Perception in itself a gain
Replying to its price;
The Object Absolute is nought,
Perception sets it fair,
And then upbraids a Perfectness
That situates so far.

XV.

NO other can reduce
      Our mortal consequence,
Like the remembering it be nought
A period from hence.
But contemplation for
Contemporaneous nought
Our single competition;
Jehovah's estimate.

XVI.

THE blunder is to estimate,–
        "Eternity is *Then*,"
We say, as of a station.
Meanwhile he is so near,
He joins me in my ramble,
Divides abode with me,
No friend have I that so persists
And this Eternity.

XVII.

MY Wheel is in the dark,–
        I cannot see a spoke,
Yet know its dripping feet
Go round and round.

My foot is on the tide –
An unfrequented road,
Yet have all roads
A "clearing" at the end.

Some have resigned the Loom,
Some in the busy tomb
Find quaint employ,
Some with new, stately feet
Pass royal through the gate,
Flinging the problem back at you and I.

XVIII.

THERE is another Loneliness
    That many die without,
Not want or friend occasions it,
Or circumstances or lot.

But nature sometimes, sometimes thought,
As whoso it befall
Is richer than could be divulged
By mortal numeral.

XIX.

SO gay a flower bereaved the mind
    As if it were a woe,
Is Beauty an affliction, then?
Tradition ought to know.

XX.

GLORY is that bright tragic thing,
    That for an instant
Means Dominion,
Warms some poor name
That never felt the sun,
Gently replacing
In oblivion.

XXI.

THE missing All prevented me
　　From missing minor things.
If nothing larger than a World's
Departure from a hinge,
Or Sun's extinction be observed,
'T was not so large that I
Could lift my forehead from my work
For curiosity.

XXII.

HIS mind, of man a secret makes,
　　I meet him with a start,
He carries a circumference
In which I have no part,
Or even if I deem I do —
He otherwise may know.
Impregnable to inquest,
However neighborly.

XXIII.

THE suburbs of a secret
    A strategist should keep,
Better than on a dream intrude
To scrutinize the sleep.

XXIV.

THE difference between despair
    And fear, is like the one
Between the instant of a wreck,
Ad when the wreck has been.

The mind is smooth,–no motion–
Contented as the eye
Upon the forehead of a Bust,
That knows it cannot see.

XXV.

THERE is a solitude of space,
    A solitude of sea,
A solitude of death, but these
Society shall be,
Compared with that profounder site,
That polar privacy,
A Soul admitted to Itself:
Finite Infinity.

XXVI.

THE props assist the house
　　　Until the house is built,
And then the props withdraw –
And adequate, erect,
The house supports itself;
Ceasing to recollect
The auger and the carpenter.
Just such a retrospect
Hath the perfected life,
A past of plank and nail,
And slowness, – then the scaffolds drop –
Affirming it a soul.

XXVII.

THE gleam of an heroic act,
　　　Such strange illumination –
The Possible's slow fuse is lit
By the Imagination!

XXVIII.

OF Death the sharpest function,
        That, just as we discern,
The Excellence defies us;
Securest gathered then
The fruit perverse to plucking,
But leaning to the sight
With the ecstatic limit
Of unobtained Delight.

XXIX.

DOWN Time's quaint stream
        Without an oar,
We are enforced to sail,
Our Port—a secret—
Our Perchance—a gale.
What Skipper would
Incur the risk,
What Buccaneer would ride,
Without a surety from the wind
Or schedule of the tide?

XXX.

I BET with every Wind that blew, till Nature
        in chagrin
Employed a *Fact* to visit me and scuttle my
        Balloon!

XXXI.

THE Future never spoke,
        Nor will he, like the Dumb,
Reveal by sign or syllable
Of his profound To-come.
But when the news be ripe,
Presents it in the Act—
Forestalling preparation
Escape or substitute.
Indifferent to him
The Dower as the Doom,
His office but to execute
Fate's Telegram to him.

XXXII.

TWO lengths has every day,
        Its absolute extent—
And area superior
By hope or heaven lent.
Eternity will be
Velocity, or pause,
At fundamental signals
From fundamental laws.
To die, is not to go—
On doom's consummate chart
No territory new is staked,
Remain thou as thou art.

XXXIII.

THE Soul's superior instants
      Occur to Her alone,
When friend and earth's occasion
Have infinite withdrawn.

Or she, Herself, ascended
To too remote a height,
For lower recognition
Than Her Omnipotent.

This mortal abolition
Is seldom, but as fair
As Apparition – subject
To autocratic air.

Eternity's disclosure
To favorites, a few,
Of the Colossal substance
Of immortality.

XXXIV.

NATURE is what we see,
      The Hill, the Afternoon –
Squirrel, Eclipse, the Bumble-bee,
Nay – Nature is Heaven.

Nature is what we hear,
The Bobolink, the Sea –
Thunder, the Cricket –
Nay, – Nature is Harmony.

Nature is what we know
But have no art to say,
So impotent our wisdom is
To Her simplicity.

XXXV.

AH, Teneriffe!
                    Retreating
Mountain!
Purples of Ages pause for you,
Sunset reviews her Sapphire Regiment,
Day drops you her red Adieu!

Still, clad in your mail of ices,
Thigh of granite and thew of steel –
Heedless, alike, of pomp or parting,
Ah, Teneriffe!
                    I'm kneeling still.

XXXVI.

SHE died at play
            Gambolled away
Her lease of spotted hours,
Then sank as gaily as a Turk
Upon a couch of flowers.
Her ghost strolled softly o'er the hill
Yesterday and today,
Her vestments as the silver fleece,
Her countenance as spray.

XXXVII.

"MORNING" means "Milking" to the
        Farmer,
Dawn to the Apennines—
Dice to the Maid.
"Morning" means just Chance to the Lover—
Just Revelation to the Beloved.
Epicures date a breakfast by it!
Heroes a battle,
The Miller a flood,
Faint-going eyes their lapse
From sighing,
Faith, the Experiment of our Lord!

XXXVIII.

A LITTLE madness in the Spring
        Is wholesome even for the King,
But God be with the Clown,
Who ponders this tremendous scene—
This whole experiment of green,
As if it were his own!

XXXIX.

I CAN'T tell you, but you feel it —
         Nor can you tell me,
Saints with vanished slate and pencil
Solve our April day.

Sweeter than a vanished Frolic
From a vanished Green!
Swifter than the hoofs of Horsemen
Round a ledge of Dream!

Modest, let us walk among it,
With our "faces veiled,"
As they say polite Archangels
Do, in meeting God.

Not for *me* to prate about it,
Not for *you* to say
To some fashionable Lady —
"Charming April Day!"

Rather Heaven's "Peter Parley,"
By which, Children — slow —
To sublimer recitations
Are prepared to go!

XL.

SOME Days retired from the rest
　　In soft distinction lie,
The Day that a companion came —
Or was obliged to die.

XLI.

LIKE Men and Women shadows walk
　　Upon the hills today,
With here and there a mighty bow,
Or trailing courtesy
To Neighbors, doubtless, of their own;
Not quickened to perceive
Minuter landscape, as Ourselves
And Boroughs where we live.

XLII.

THE butterfly obtains
　　But little sympathy,
Though favorably mentioned
In Entomology.
Because he travels freely
And wears a proper coat,
The circumspect are certain
That he is dissolute.
Had he the homely scutcheon of modest Industry,
'T were fitter certifying for Immortality.

XLIII.

BEAUTY crowds me till I die,
        Beauty, mercy have on me!
But if I expire today,
Let it be in sight of thee.

XLIV.

WE spy the Forests and the Hills,
        The tents to Nature's Show,
Mistake the outside for the in
And mention what we saw.

Could Commentators on the sign
Of Nature's Caravan
Obtain "admission," as a child,
Some Wednesday afternoon?

XLIV.

I NEVER told the buried gold
      Upon the hill that lies,
I saw the sun, his plunder done,
Crouch low to guard his prize.

He stood as near, as stood you here,
A pace had been between—
Did but a snake bisect the brake,
My life had forfeit been.

That was a wondrous booty,
I hope 't was honest gained—
Those were the finest ingots
That ever kissed the spade.

Whether to keep the secret—
Whether to reveal—
Whether, while I ponder
Kidd may sudden sail—

Could a Shrewd advise me
We might e'en divide—
Should a Shrewd betray me—
"Atropos" decide!

XLVI.

THE largest fire ever known
      Occurs each afternoon,
Discovered is without surprise,
Proceeds without concern:
Consumes, and no report to men,
An Occidental town,
Rebuilt another morning
To be again burned down.

XLVII.

BLOOM upon the Mountain, stated,
      Blameless of a name.
Efflorescence of a Sunset—
Reproduced, the same.

Seed, had I, my purple sowing
Should endow the Day,
Not a tropic of the twilight
Show itself away.

Who for tilling, to the Mountain
Come, and disappear—
Whose be Her renown, or fading,
Witness, is not here.

While I state—the solemn petals
Far as North and East,
Far as South and West expanding,
Culminate in rest.

And the Mountain to the Evening
Fit His countenance,
Indicating by no muscle
The Experience.

XLVIII.

MARCH is the month of expectation,
     The things we do not know,
The Persons of prognostication
Are coming now.
We try to sham becoming firmness,
But pompous joy
Betrays us, as his first betrothal
Betrays a boy.

XLIX.

THE Duties of the Wind are few —
      To cast the Ships at sea,
Establish March,
The Floods escort,
And usher Liberty.

L.

THE Winds drew off
      Like hungry dogs
Defeated of a bone.
Through fissures in
Volcanic cloud
The yellow lightning shown.
The trees held up
Their mangled limbs
Like animals in pain,
When Nature falls
Upon herself,
Beware an Austrian!

LI.

I THINK that the root of the Wind is Water,
        It would not sound so deep
Were it a firmamental product,
Airs no Oceans keep—
Mediterranean intonations,
To a Current's ear
There is a maritime conviction
In the atmosphere.

LII.

SO, from the mould,
        Scarlet and gold
Many a Bulb will rise,
Hidden away cunningly
From sagacious eyes.
So, from cocoon
Many a Worm
Leap so Highland gay,
Peasants like me—
Peasants like thee,
Gaze perplexedly.

LIII.

THE long sigh of the Frog
        Upon a Summer's day,
Enacts intoxication
Upon the revery.
But his receding swell
Substantiates a peace,
That makes the ear inordinate
For corporal release.

LIV.

A CAP of lead across the sky
        Was tight and surly drawn,
We could not find the mighty Face,
The Figure was withdrawn.

A chill came up as from a shaft,
Our noon became a well,
A Thunder storm combines the charms
Of Winter and of Hell.

LV.

I SEND two Sunsets—
        Day and I in competition ran,
I finished two, and several stars,
While He was making one.

His own is ampler—
But, as I was saying to a friend,
Mine is the more convenient
To carry in the hand.

LVI.

OF this is Day composed—
        A morning and a noon,
A Revelry unspeakable
And then a gay Unknown;
Whose Pomps allure and spurn—
And dower and deprive,
And penury for glory
Remedilessly leave.

LVII.

THE Hills erect their purple heads,
    The Rivers lean to see —
Yet Man has not, of all the throng,
A curiosity.

LVIII.

LIGHTLY stepped a yellow star
    To its lofty place,
Loosed the Moon her silver hat
From her lustral face.
All of evening softly lit
As an astral hall —
"Father," I observed to Heaven,
"You are punctual."

LIX.

THE Moon upon her fluent route
    Defiant of a road,
The stars Etruscan argument,
Substantiate a God.
If Aims impel these Astral Ones,
The Ones allowed to know,
Know that which makes them as forgot
As Dawn forgets them now.

LX.

LIKE some old fashioned miracle
          When Summertime is done,
Seems Summer's recollection
And the affairs of June.

As infinite tradition
As Cinderella's bays,
Or little John of Lincoln Green,
Or Bluebeard's galleries.

Her Bees have a fictitious hum,
Her Blossoms, like a dream,
Elate – until we almost weep
So plausible they seem.

Her Memories like strains – review –
When Orchestra is dumb,
The Violin in baize replaced
And Ear and Heaven numb.

LXI.

GLOWING is her Bonnet,
    Glowing is her Cheek,
Glowing is her Kirtle,
Yet she cannot speak!

Better, as the Daisy
From the Summer hill,
Vanish unrecorded,
Save by tearful Rill,

Save by loving Sunrise
Looking for her face,
Save by feet unnumbered
Pausing at the place!

LXII.

FOREVER cherished by the tree,
    Whose apple Winter warm,
Enticed to breakfast from the sky
Two Gabriels yestermorn;
They registered in Nature's book
As Robin – Sire and Son,
But angels have that modest way
To screen them from renown.

LXIII.

THE Ones that disappeared are back,
    The Phoebe and the Crow,
Precisely as in March is heard
The curtness of the Jay—
Be this an Autumn or a Spring?
My wisdom loses way,
One side of me the nuts are ripe—
The other side is May.

LXIV.

THOSE final Creatures,—who they are—
    That, faithful to the close,
Administer her ecstasy,
But just the Summer knows.

LXV.

SUMMER begins to have the look,
        Peruser of enchanting Book
Reluctantly, but sure, perceives—
A gain upon the backward leaves.

Autumn begins to be inferred
By millinery of the cloud,
Or deeper color in the shawl
That wraps the everlasting hill.

The eye begins its avarice,
A meditation chastens speech,
Some Dyer of a distant tree
Resumes his gaudy industry.

Conclusion is the course of all,
Almost to be perennial,
And then elude stability
Recalls to immortality.

LXVI.

A PROMPT, executive Bird is the Jay,
        Bold as a Bailiff's hymn,
Brittle and brief in quality—
Warrant in every line;
Sitting a bough like a Brigadier,
Confident and straight,
Much is the mien
Of him in March
As a Magistrate.

LXVII.

LIKE brooms of steel
      The Snow and Wind
Had swept the Winter Street,
The House was hooked,
The Sun sent out
Faint Deputies of heat—
Where rode the Bird
The Silence tied
His ample, plodding Steed,
The Apple in the cellar snug
Was all the one that played.

LXVIII.

THESE are the days that Reindeer love
      And pranks the Northern star,
This is the Sun's objective
And Finland of the year.

LXIX.

FOLLOW wise Orion
      Till you lose your eye,
Dazzlingly decamping
He is just as high.

LXX.

IN Winter, in my room,
　　I came upon a worm,
Pink, lank, and warm.
But as he was a worm
And worms presume,
Not quite with him at home –
Secured him by a string
To something neighboring,
And went along.

A trifle afterward
A thing occurred,
I'd not believe it if I heard –
But state with creeping blood;
A snake, with mottles rare,
Surveyed my chamber floor,
In feature as the worm
before,
But ringed with power.
The very string
With which I tied him, too,
When he was mean and new,
That string was there.

I shrank –"How fair you are!"
Propitiation's claw –
"Afraid," he hissed,
"Of me?"
"No cordiality?"
He fathomed me.

Then, to a rhythm slim
Secreted in his form,
As patterns swim,
Projected him.

That time I flew,
Both eyes his way,
Lest he pursue –
Nor ever ceased to run,
Till, in a distant town,
Towns on from mine –
I sat me down;
This was a dream.

LXXI.

NOT any sunny tone
        From any fervent zone
Finds entrance there.
Better a grave of Balm
Toward human nature's home,
And Robins near,
Than a stupendous Tomb
Proclaiming to the gloom
How dead we are.

LXXII.

FOR Death,—or rather
           For the things 't will buy,
These put away
Life's opportunity.
The things that Death will buy
Are Room,—Escape
From Circumstances,
And a Name.
How gifts of Life
With Death's gifts will compare,
We know not—
For the rates stop Here.

LXXIII.

DROPPED into the
           Ether Acre!
Wearing the sod gown—
Bonnet of Everlasting laces—
Brooch frozen on!
Horses of blonde—
And coach of silver,
Baggage a strapped Pearl!
Journey of Down
And whip of Diamond—
Riding to meet the Earl!

LXXIV.

THIS quiet Dust was Gentlemen and Ladies,
    And Lads and Girls;
Was laughter and ability and sighing,
    And frocks and curls.
This passive place a Summer's nimble mansion,
    Where Bloom and Bees
Fulfilled their Oriental Circuit,
    Then ceased like these.

LXXV.

'TWAS comfort in her dying room
    To hear the living clock,
A short relief to have the wind
Walk boldly up and knock,
Diversion from the dying theme
To hear the children play,
But wrong, the mere
That these could live,—
And This of ours must die!

LXXVI.

TOO cold is this
        To warm with sun,
Too stiff to bended be,
To joint this agate were a feat
Outstaring masonry.
How went the agile kernel out—
Contusion of the husk,
Nor rip, nor wrinkle indicate,—
But just an Asterisk.

LXXXVII.

I WATCHED her face to see which way
        She took the awful news,
Whether she died before she heard—
Or in protracted bruise
Remained a few short years with us,
Each heavier than the last—
A further afternoon to fail,
As Flower at fall of Frost.

LXXVIII.

TODAY or this noon
       She dwelt so close,
I almost touched her;
Tonight she lies
Past neighborhood —
And bough and steeple —
Now past surmise.

LXXXIX.

I SEE thee better in the dark,
       I do not need a light.
The love of thee a prism be
Excelling violet.

I see thee better for the years
That hunch themselves between,
The miner's lamp sufficient be
To nullify the mine.

And in the grave I see thee best —
Its little panels be
A-glow, all ruddy with the light
I held so high for thee!

What need of day to those whose dark
Hath so surpassing sun,
It seem it be continually
At the meridian?

LXXXI.

LOW at my problem bending,
        Another problem comes,
Larger than mine, serener,
Involving statelier sums;
I check my busy pencil,
My ciphers slip away,
Wherefore, my baffled fingers,
Time Eternity?

LXXXI.

IF pain for peace prepares,
        Lo the "Augustan" years
Our feet await!

If Springs from Winter rise,
Can the Anemone's
Be reckoned up?

If night stands first, then noon,
To gird us for the sun,
What gaze —

When, from a thousand skies,
On our developed eyes
Noons blaze!

LXXXII.

I FIT for them,
        I seek the dark till I am thorough fit.
The labor is a solemn one,
With this sufficient sweet—
That abstinence as mine produce
A purer good for them,
If I succeed,—
If not, I had
The transport of the Aim.

LXXXIII.

NOT one by Heaven defrauded stay,
        Although He seem to steal,
He restitutes in some sweet way.
Secreted in His will.

LXXXIV.

THE feet of people walking home
    In gayer sandals go,
The Crocus, till she rises,
The Vassal of the Snow—
The lips at Hallelujah!
Long years of practice bore,
Till bye and bye these Bargemen
Walked singing on the shore.

Pearls are the Diver's farthings
Extorted from the Sea,
Pinions the Seraph's wagon,
Pedestrians once, as we—
Night is the morning's canvas,
Larceny, legacy,
Death but our rapt attention
To immortality.

My figures fail to tell me
How far the village lies,
Whose Peasants are the angels,
Whose Cantons dot the skies,
My Classics veil their faces,
My Faith that dark adores,
Which from its solemn Abbeys
Such resurrection pours!

LXXXV.

WE should not mind so small a flower,
       Except it quiet bring
Our little garden that we lost
Back to the lawn again.
So spicy her Carnations red,
So drunken reel her Bees,
So silver steal a hundred Flutes
From out a hundred trees,
That whoso sees this little flower,
By faith may clear behold
The Bobolinks around the throne,
And Dandelions gold.

LXXXVI.

TO the staunch Dust we safe commit thee;
       Tongue if it hath, inviolate to thee—
Silence denote and Sanctity enforce thee,
Passenger of Infinity!

LXXXVII.

HER "Last Poems"–
      Poets ended,
Silver perished with her tongue,
Not on record bubbled other
Flute, or Woman, so divine;
Not unto its Summer morning
Robin uttered half the tune–
Gushed too free for the adoring,
From the Anglo-Florentine.
Late the praise–
'T is dull conferring
On a Head too high to crown,
Diadem or Ducal showing,
Be its Grave sufficient sign.
Yet if we, no Poet's kinsman,
Suffocate with easy woe,
What and if ourself a Bridegroom,
Put Her down, in Italy?

LXXXVIII.

IMMURED in Heaven! What a Cell!
      Let every bondage be,
Thou Sweetest of the Universe,
Like that which ravished thee!

LXXXIX.

I'M thinking of that other morn,
    When Cerements let go,
And Creatures clad in Victory
Go up in two by two!

XC.

THE overtakelessness of those
    Who have accomplished Death,
Majestic is to me beyond
The majesties of Earth.

The soul her "not at Home"
Inscribes upon the flesh,
And takes her fair aerial gait
Beyond the hope of touch.

XCI.

THE Look of Thee, what is it like?
　　Hast thou a hand or foot,
Or mansion of Identity,
And what is thy Pursuit?

Thy fellows,—are they Realms or Themes?
Hast thou Delight or Fear
Or Longing,—and is that for us
Or values more severe?

Let change transfuse all other traits,
Enact all other blame,
But deign this least certificate—
That thou shalt be the same.

XCII.

THE Devil, had he fidelity,
　　Would be the finest friend—
Because he has ability,
But Devils cannot mend.
Perfidy is the virtue
That would he but resign,—
The Devil, so amended,
Were durably divine.

XCIII.

PAPA above!
     Regard a Mouse
O'erpowered by the Cat;
Reserve within thy kingdom
A "mansion" for the Rat!

Snug in seraphic cupboards
To nibble all the day,
While unsuspecting cycles
Wheel pompously away.

XCIV.

NOT when we know
     The Power accosts,
The garment of Surprise
Was all our timid Mother wore
At Home, in Paradise.

XCV.

ELIJAH'S wagon knew no thill,
     Was innocent of wheel,
Elijah's horses as unique
As was his vehicle.
Elijah's journey to portray,
Expire with him the skill,
Who justified Elijah,
In feats inscrutable.

XCVI.

"REMEMBER me," implored the Thief—
      Oh magnanimity!
"My Visitor in Paradise
I give thee Guaranty."

That courtesy will fair remain,
When the delight is dust,
With which we cite this mightiest case
Of compensated Trust.

Of All, we are allowed to hope,
But Affidavit stands
That this was due, where some, we fear,
Are unexpected friends.

XCVII.

TO this apartment deep
      No ribaldry may creep;
Untroubled this abode
By any man but God.

XCVIII.

"SOWN in dishonor?"
        Ah! Indeed!
May this dishonor be?
If I were half so fine myself,
I'd notice nobody!

"Sown in corruption?"
By no means!
Apostle is askew;
Corinthians I.I5, narrates
A circumstance or two!

XCIX.

WHO is it seeks my pillow nights?
        With plain inspecting face,
"Did you, or did you not?" to ask,
'T is Conscience, childhood's nurse.

With martial hand she strokes the hair
Upon my wincing head,
"All rogues shall have their part in"–
What–
        The Phosphorus of God.

C.

HIS Cheek is his Biographer—
        As long as he can blush,
Perdition is Opprobrium;
Past that, he sins in peace.

CI.

"HEAVENLY Father," take to thee
        The supreme iniquity,
Fashioned by thy candid hand
In a moment contraband.
Though to trust us seem to us
More respectful—"we are dust."
We apologize to Thee
For Thine own Duplicity.

CII.

THE sweets of Pillage can be known
        To no one but the Thief,
Compassion for Integrity
Is his divinest Grief.

CIII.

A LITTLE over Jordan,
       As Genesis record,
An Angel and a Wrestler
Did wrestle long and hard.

Till, morning touching mountain,
And Jacob waxing strong,
The Angel begged permission
To breakfast and return.

Not so, quoth wily Jacob
And grit his loins anew,
"Until thou bless me, stranger!"
The which acceded to:

Light swung the silver fleeces
Peniel hills among,
And the astonished Wrestler
Found he had worsted God!

CIV.

DUST is the only secret,
　　Death the only one
You cannot find out all about
In his native town:
Nobody knew his father,
Never was a boy,
Had n't any playmates
Or early history.

Industrious, laconic,
Punctual, sedate,
Bolder than a Brigand,
Swifter than a Fleet,
Builds like a bird too,
Christ robs the nest —
Robin after robin
Smuggled to rest!

CV.

AMBITION cannot find him,
　　Affection doesn't know
How many leagues of Nowhere
Lie between them now.
Yesterday undistinguished —
Eminent today,
For our mutual honor —
Immortality!

CVI.

EDEN is that old fashioned House
        We dwell in every day,
Without suspecting our abode
Until we drive away.
How fair, on looking back, the Day
We sauntered from the door,
Unconscious our returning
Discover it no more.

CVII.

CANDOR, my tepid Friend,
        Come not to play with me!
The Myrrhs and Mochas of the Mind
Are its Iniquity.

CVIII.

SPEECH is a symptom of affection,
        And Silence one,
The perfectest communication
Is heard of none —
Exists and its indorsement
Is had within —
Behold! said the Apostle,
Yet had not seen.

CIX.

WHO were "the Father and the Son" –
    We pondered when a child,
And what had they to do with us –
And when portentous told
With inference appalling,
By Childhood fortified,
We thought, "at least they are no worse
Than they have been described."

Who are "the Father and the Son" –
Did we demand today,
"The Father and the Son" himself
Would doubtless specify,
But had they the felicity
When we desired to know,
We better Friends had been, perhaps,
Than time ensue to be.

We start, to learn that we believe
But once, entirely –
Belief, it does not fit so well
When altered frequently.
We blush, that Heaven if we achieve,
Event ineffable –
We shall have shunned, until ashamed
To own the Miracle.

CX.

THAT Love is all there is,
        Is all we know of Love;
It is enough, the freight should be
Proportioned to the groove.

CXI.

THE luxury to apprehend
        The luxury 't would be
To look at thee a single time,
An Epicure of me,
In whatsoever Presence, makes,
Till, for a further food
I scarcely recollect to starve,
So first am I supplied.
The luxury to meditate
The luxury it was
To banquet on thy Countenance,
A sumptuousness bestows
On plainer days,
Whose table, far as
Certainly can see,
Is laden with a single crumb —
The consciousness of Thee.

CXII.

THE Sea said "Come" to the Brook,
        The Brook said "Let me grow!"
The Sea said "Then you will be a Sea—
I want a brook, Come now!"

CXIII.

ALL I may, if small,
        Do it not display
Larger for its Totalness?
'T is economy
To bestow a world
And withhold a star,
Utmost is munificence;
Less, though larger, Poor.

CXIV.

LOVE reckons by itself alone,
        "As large as I" relate the Sun
To one who never felt it blaze,
Itself is all the like it has.

CXV.

THE inundation of the Spring
      Submerges every soul,
It sweeps the tenement away
But leaves the water whole.
In which the Soul, at first alarmed,
Seeks furtive for its shore,
But acclimated, gropes no more
For that Peninsular.

CXVI.

NO Autumn's intercepting chill
      Appalls this Tropic Beast,
But African exuberance
And Asiatic rest.

CXVII.

VOLCANOES be in Sicily
      And South America,
I judge from my geography.
Volcanoes nearer here,
A lava step, at any time,
Am I inclined to climb,
A crater I may contemplate,
Vesuvius at home.

CXVIII.

DISTANCE is not the realm of Fox,
    Nor by relay as Bird;
Abated, Distance is until
Thyself, Beloved!

CXIX.

THE treason of an accent
    Might vilify the Joy —
To breathe, — corrode the rapture
Of Sanctity to be.

CXX.

HOW destitute is he
    Whose Gold is firm,
Who finds it every time,
The small stale sum —
When Love, with but a pence
Will so display,
As is a disrespect to India!

CXXI.

CRISIS is sweet and, set the Heart
            Upon the hither side,
Has dowers of prospective
Surrendered by the Tried.
Inquire of the closing Rose
Which Rapture she preferred,
And she will tell you, sighing,
The transport of the Bud.

CXXII.

TO tell the beauty would decrease,
            To state the Spell demean,
There is a syllableless sea
Of which it is the sign.

My will endeavours for its word
And fails, but entertains
A rapture as of legacies –
Of introspective mines.

CXXIII.

TO love thee, year by year,
            May less appear
Than sacrifice and cease.
However, Dear,
Forever might be short
I thought, to show,
And so I pieced it with a flower now.

CXXIV.

I SHOWED her heights she never saw—
        "Would'st climb?" I said,
She said "Not so"—
"With me?" I said, "With me?"
I showed her secrets
Morning's nest,
The rope that Nights were put across—
And *now*, "Would 'st have me for a
Guest?"
She could not find her yes—
And then, I brake my life, and Lo!
A light for her, did solemn glow,
The larger, as her face withdrew—
And could she, further, "No"?

CXXV.

ON my volcano grows the grass,—
        A meditative spot,
An area for a bird to choose
Would be the general thought.

How red the fire reeks below,
How insecure the sod—
Did I disclose, would populate
With awe my solitude.

CXXVI.

IF I could tell how glad I was,
        I should not be so glad,
But when I cannot make the Force
Nor mould it into word,
I know it is a sign
That new Dilemma be
From mathematics further off,
Than from Eternity.

CXXVII.

HER Grace is all she has,
        And that, so vast displays,
One Art, to recognize, must be,
Another Art to praise.

CXXVIII.

NO matter where the Saints abide,
        They make their circuit fair;
Behold how great a Firmament
Accompanies a star!

CXXIX.

TO see her is a picture,
        To hear her is a tune,
To know her an intemperance
As innocent as June;
By which to be undone
Is dearer than Redemption —
Which never to receive,
Makes mockery of melody
It might have been to live.

CXXX.

SO set its sun in thee,
        What day is dark to me —
What distance far,
So I the ships may see
That touch how seldomly
Thy shore?

CXXXI.

HAD this one day not been,
        Or could it cease to be —
How smitten, how superfluous
Were every other day!

Lest Love should value less
What Loss would value more,
Had it the stricken privilege —
It cherishes before.

CXXXII.

THAT she forgot me was the least,
        I felt it second pain,
That I was worthy to forget
Was most I thought upon.

Faithful, was all that I could boast,
But Constancy became,
To her, by her innominate,
A something like a shame.

CXXXIII.

THE incidents of Love
        Are more than its Events,
Investments best expositor
Is the minute per cents.

CXXXIV.

JUST so, Jesus raps—He does not weary—
        Last at the knocker and first at the bell,
Then on divinest tiptoe standing
Might He out-spy the lady's soul
When He retires, chilled and weary—
It will be ample time for me;
Patient, upon the steps, until then—
Heart, I am knocking low at Thee!

CXXXV.

SAFE Despair it is that raves,
    Agony is frugal,
Puts itself severe away
For its own perusual.

Garrisoned no Soul can be
In the front of Trouble,
Love is one, not aggregate,
Nor is Dying double.

CXXXVI.

THE Face we choose to miss,
    Be it but for a day—
As absent as a hundred years
When it has rode away.

OF so divine a loss
    We enter but the gain,
Indemnity for loneliness
That such a bliss has been.

EMILY DICKINSON

CXXXVIII.

THE healed Heart shows its shallow scar
      With confidential moan,
Not mended by Mortality
Are fabrics truly torn.
To go its convalescent way
So shameless is to see,
More genuine were Perfidy
Than such Fidelity.

CXXXIX.

TO pile like Thunder to its close,
      Then crumble grand away,
While everything created hid –
This would be Poetry:
Or Love, – the two coeval came –
We both and neither prove,
Experience either, and consume –
For none see God and live.

CXL.

THE Stars are old, that stood for me—
    The West a little worn,
Yet newer glows the only Gold
I ever cared to earn—
Presuming on that lone result
Her infinite disdain,
But vanquished her with my defeat,
'Twas Victory was slain.

CXLI.

ALL circumstances are the frame
    In which His Face is set,
All Latitudes exist for His
Sufficient continent.

The light His Action and the dark
The Leisure of His Will,
In Him Existence serve, or set
A force illegible.

CXLII.

I DID not reach thee,
    But my feet slip nearer every day;
Three Rivers and a Hill to cross,
One Desert and a Sea –
I shall not count the journey one
When I am telling thee.

Two deserts – but the year is cold
So that will help the sand –
One desert crossed, the second one
Will feel as cool as land.
Sahara is too little price
To pay for thy Right hand!

The sea comes last. Step merry, feet!
So short have we to go
To play together we are prone,
But we must labor now,
The last shall be the lightest load
That we have to draw.

The Sun goes crooked – that is night –
Before he makes the bend
We must have passed the middle sea,
Almost we wish the end
Were further off – too great it seems
So near the Whole to stand.

We step like plush, we stand like snow—
The waters murmur now,
Three rivers and the hill are passed,
Two deserts and the sea!
Now Death usurps my premium
And gets the look at Thee.

. . .

Essays

Emily Dickinson

BY

THORNTON WILDER

AS A POET Emily Dickinson started out with two great
disadvantages – an enormous facility for versifying and
an infatuation with bad models. Later she was to read
absorbedly Shakespeare, Milton, Herbert, and the great English
poets of her century, and one is aware of the influence they had
upon her language, but one is also aware of how little an effect
they had upon the verse forms she employed. Her point of
departure was the lyric of the keepsake and the Christmas
Annual and the newspaper and the genteel periodical – the
avocation of clergymen and of ladies of refinement and
sensibility. Even the better poets of the hymnbooks do not seem
to have greatly influenced her. Although she was to make some
startling innovations within this form, it is no less startling that
she made no attempts to depart from the half-dozen stanzaic
patterns with which she began. I choose to see in this fact an
additional illustration of that *arrest* in her development which
we have discovered elsewhere. She was extraordinarily bold in
what she did within these patterns (she soon *burst their seams),*
but the form of the poem and to some extent the kind of poem
she admired as a girl continued to be the poem she wrote to
the end.

She wrote to Colonel Higginson in April, 1862 (she was then
thirty-one years old): "I made no verse, but one or two, until
last winter, sir." So far, very few poems have been, with
assurance, dated prior to that time; but it seems to me that she
here intended the qualification: no verse of the highest

conscious intention. There are numbers of poems of about this time, and certainly early (hence, naturally, the darlings of the anthologists), such as "If I Can Stop One Heart from Breaking" and "I Taste a Liquor Never Brewed" and "To Fight Aloud Is Very Brave," which show evidence of having been preceded by a long experience in versifying. The passage from one stanza to the next is very accomplished indeed, and presupposes an extended practice, in public or in private. It appears certain to me that when, toward 1861, Emily Dickinson collected herself to write verse of the most earnest intention, she had to struggle not only against the pitfalls of a native facility, but against those of a facility already long exercised in a superficial effectiveness – in the easy pathos and in the easy epigram.

Even before she sent the first examples of her work to Colonel Higginson she had won a critical battle over her facility. She had found the courage to write poetry which "insulted the intelligence" of her contemporaries. What shocked Colonel Higginson was not that she occasionally employed "bad" rhymes (such abounded in the poetry of Mrs. Browning); nor that she substituted assonance for rhyme; nor even that she occasionally failed to rhyme at all (that practice he had accepted in Walt Whitman, whose work he recommended to her reading); but that all these irregularities were combined and deeply embedded in most conventional of all verse forms.

At this distance we can venture to reconstruct her struggles. A new tide had entered her being; she now wished to say with passion what she had been hitherto saying playfully, saying with coquetry. New intensities – particularly in new countries – call for new forms. A childhood fixation, however, prevented her from abandoning the stanzaic patterns of her early reading. She revolted from the regular rhyme, the eternal "my-die" and "God-rod," not because she was too lazy to impose it, but because the regular rhyme seemed the outer expression of an inner conventionality. She called the regular rhyme "prose"–"they shut me up in prose"–and in the same poem she calls it "captivity."

One of her devices shows us how conscious she was of what she was doing. She artfully offers us rhymes of increasing regularity so that our ear will be waiting for another, and then in a concluding verse refuses any rhyme whatever. The poem "Of Tribulation These Are They" gives us "white-designate," "times-palms," "soil-mile," "road-*Saved!*" (The italics are hers.) The effect is as of a ceiling being removed from above our heads. The incommensurable invades the poem. In "I'll Tell Thee All–How Blank It Grew" she flings all the windows open in closing with the words "outvisions paradise," rhymeless after three stanzas of unusually regular rhymes.

Her "teacher" rebuked her for these audacities, but she persisted in them. She did not stoop to explain or defend them. The Colonel's unwillingness to publish the work showed her that he did not consider her a poet, however much he may have been struck by individual phrases. She continued to enclose an occasional poem in her letters to friends, but they seem not to have asked to see "lots of them." The hope of encouragement and the thought of a contemporary audience grew more and more remote. Yet the possibility of a literary fame, of an ultimate glory, never ceased to trouble her. In poem after poem she derided renown; she compared it to an auction and to the croaking of frogs; but at the same time she hailed it as this consecration of the poet's "vital light." What did she do about it? She took five steps forward and two steps back. It is no inconsiderable advance toward literary pretension to write two thousand poems; yet the condition in which she left them is a no less conspicuous retreat. She called on posterity to witness that she was indifferent to its approval, but she did not destroy her work. She did not even destroy the "sweepings of the studio," the tentative sketches at the margin of the table. Had she left fair copies, the movement would have been five steps forward and one step back; had she directed that the work be burned by others, it would have been three steps back.

I am convinced that she went even further in her wish to appear indifferent to our good opinion; she deliberately marred many a poem; she did not so much insult our intelligence as flout it. As we read the more authentic work we are astonished to find that poem after poem concludes with some lapse into banality, or begins flatly and mounts to splendor. No one would claim that she was free of lapses of judgment and of taste, but the last three words of "How Many Times These Low Feet Staggered" or the last verse of "They Put Us Far Apart" are, poetically speaking, of an almost insolent cynicism – the first for flatness, the second for cacophony.

That is to say, Emily Dickinson frequently wrote badly *on purpose*. She did not aspire to your praise and mine, if we were the kind of persons who cannot distinguish the incidental from the essential. She had withdrawn a long way from our human, human, human, discriminations and judgments. As we have seen, she was singed, if not scorched, in early life by the all-too-human in her family relationships. Thereafter she was abandoned – "betrayed" she called it – by the person (or as I prefer to see it, by the succession of persons) whom most she loved. She withdrew from us: into her house; and even in her house she withdrew – the few old friends who came to call were required to converse with her through a half-open door. She became more and more abstract in her view of people. She did not repudiate us entirely, but she increasingly cherished the thought that we would all be more estimable when we were dead. She was capable of envisaging the fact that there may be no life hereafter: "Their Height in Heaven Comforts Not" acknowledges that the whole matter is a "house of supposition . . . that skirts the acres of perhaps." But only such a company, unencumbered with earthly things, would understand what she was saying, and she took ample pains to discourage all others. The poem that begins "Some work for Immortality, the chiefer part for *Time*," is not primarily about books sold in bookstores.

Thornton Wilder (1897–1975), American writer, won Pulitzer Prizes for the novel *The Bridge of San Luis Rey* and the plays *Our Town* and *The Skin of Our Teeth*.

Emily Dickinson and the Poetry of the Inner Life

BY

ELIZABETH JENNINGS

EMILY DICKINSON seems to have been one of those poets who have extracted the largest possible amount of material from the most outwardly meager and restricted personal experience. Yet she constructed neither a world of pure fantasy nor a series of exquisite objects which, in the manner of Marianne Moore, might be loaded with agitating emotions or pressed into an ecstatic stillness which poetry surrounds but seldom penetrates. Limited in subject-matter and in metrical cadence though they are, her poems somehow give the effect of largeness, of reverberations. The simple quatrains which Emily Dickinson usually employs seem to be not merely neat, box-like forms holding and sustaining poetic *trouvailles,* but rather delicate poetic structures which have the power of suggesting forms and cadences larger than themselves; it is as if they cast large shadows or, to change the metaphor, produced momentous and memorable echoes.

But her skill – and it is great – is not the most noticeable thing about Emily Dickinson's poetic *œuvre.* She is one of those poets who depend finally on personal honesty, on the faithful recreation of a unique experience, to make their effect. She is, briefly, completely naked to experience and lays that experience, with all the nerves exposed, before her readers.

Her subjects are few and constantly repeated – death, love, frustration, self-questioning, loneliness – but they are presented completely, entirely accessible to the reader. Emily Dickinson is also, in a very real sense, a voice rather than simply a person, and it is for this reason that she can describe experiences which might, in the hands of less painstakingly honest poets, be self-pitying or mawkish. She works at that heightened level where passion is so undiluted that it can become almost something impersonal. It is not surprising that she was a prolific poet, one who worked at white-heat, continually examining and presenting the same subjects, the same obsessions. At the very center of her work, herself both the subject and object of her poems, she wrought, out of her own highly individual and nervous self-analyses, a poetry which, paradoxically, generates a universal not a merely personal or particular passion. It is this power which places her among the major American poets.

As R.P. Blackmur has said in his study of Emily Dickinson, "The greatness of Emily Dickinson is not. . .going to be found in anybody's idea of greatness, or of Goethe, or intensity, or mysticism, or historical fatality. It is going to be found in the words she used and in the way she put them together." And, while commenting on a particular poem, he continues, "There is no forensic here, nor eloquence, nor justness; it is a bare statement amounting to vision – vision being a kind of observation of the ideal." This is fine, sensitive criticism but I would quarrel with two further comments which Blackmur has made on this poet. One is the remark, "It [one of her poems] has nothing to do with wisdom, there is no thinking in it," and the other is "success was by accident, by the mere momentum of sensibility." Now the first statement quoted above seems to be everywhere disproved in the poems themselves. They are full of "thinking" but the thinking is poetic not philosophical, and intuitive, not organized or discursive. As for Blackmur's remark about Emily Dickinson's accidental successes – this is a criticism which might fairly be leveled against any lyric poet. Blackmur is, I believe, here confusing accident with intuition, chance with suddenly discovered and surprising truth or felicity. And, furthermore, to use the word "mere" to qualify the fine phrase "momentum of sensibility" is surely to belittle all lyric poetry which works by the exercise of concentrated energy in order to find the right word, the fitting cadence. In this sense *all* lyrical poems are happy accidents but "accident," in this context, does not seem either a useful or proximate critical term; it obscures far more than it enlightens.

Nevertheless, Blackmur's study is one of the finest introductions to Emily Dickinson's poetry, largely because he is a critic who is entirely at the disposal of the poems he examines. If he blames the state of literature and religion in Emily Dickinson's own time for being the chief cause of her literary limitations, this is at least a generous judgement even if it is not one to which the cooperative reader of the poems is likely to give his full assent.

It is interesting to see, therefore, that another fine American critic, Allen Tate, approaches Emily Dickinson in a way entirely opposed to that of R.P. Blackmur. He sees the religious climate in which she lived – that of a "puritan theocracy" – as the atmosphere in which her particular kind of poetry could function most effectively. Thus he declares: "It gave an heroic proportion and a tragic mode to the experience of the individual . . . it had an immense, incalculable value for literature; it dramatized the human soul."

These are large words and perhaps they overstate their case; yet at least they gave a plausible reason why Emily Dickinson's sort of poetry could be written in the latter half of the nineteenth century in America. Such general observations about society and religion are not value judgments, they neither clarify nor annotate the poems themselves. They are, in fact, extraliterary reflections, useful scaffoldings, not pathways into the poetry. But they do clear the ground round the poems and enable the reader to examine them on their own terms.

It has been suggested already that Emily Dickinson's poems are notable for their nakedness, for their fearless presentation of

experiences which are deeply, and often painfully, personal. But
this poet was such a finely adjusted instrument for recording
experience that the findings of vision, pain or pleasure which
appear in her verse often have a universal application. And it is,
oddly enough, sometimes a kind of wry wit which makes this
generalizing power so effective, as in the following short poem:

> To hang our head ostensibly
> And subsequent, to find
> That such was not the posture
> Of our immortal mind
>
> Affords the sly presumption
> That in so dense a fuzz
> You too take cobweb attitudes
> Upon a plane of gauze.

It is difficult, I think, to see how any critic could claim that
Emily Dickinson had no *thinking* power when they have the
evidence of such a poem as this before them.

If Emily Dickinson often seems epigrammatic, even
aphoristic, her ideas and her wit are not reproving or
admonishing. She is, in one sense, always speaking to herself. It
is as if we, her readers, were privileged to overhear her
meditations and her arguments with herself. This intense poetry
in the very best sense, taut and vibrant not with emotions and
ideas which the poet has already formulated outside her poems,
but alive with the very process of thought and feeling. A vision
is thus caught on the wing, not trapped but held and halted
momentarily, just long enough for the poem to be written.

James Reeves, in his sensitive Introduction to a selection of
the poems, goes far towards explaining the nervous honesty of
Emily Dickinson's work when he says, "She did not withdraw
from the world because she hated it: there was nothing in her

of the grand romantic manner, rejecting society because the palate had become jaded. Her isolation was a calculated choice, the loss weighed against the gain, with a clear conviction of the necessity and worth of what she had to do." And again, Reeves declares, "Friends were her estate, but language was her province, and she delighted in perfecting it, whether in verse or in prose. She had what can only be called an aristocratic spirit, high-minded but without a trace of priggishness, serious without self-importance, shrewd enough to be malicious had she wished, but too gentle and kind for malice." Reeves is also eager to point out that there was nothing escapist about Emily Dickinson's attitude to life. On the contrary; if she appears to have been retiring and almost eremitical, it was because such an existence enabled her to live more fully, to face her personal predicaments with more dedication and more fearlessness. For her, language was what prayer is to the religious contemplative. She has indicated this in the following eight-line poem:

> The soul unto itself
> Is an imperial friend,
> Or the most agonising spy
> An enemy could send
>
> Secure against its own,
> No treason it can fear.
> Itself its sovereign, of itself
> The soul should stand in awe.

Emily Dickinson usually restricts herself to the quatrain or the six-line stanza, but if she thus severely limits herself in the matter of form, she compensates for this limitation by her extremely skilful use of half- and quarter-rhymes and also by her extraordinarily apt and original handling of language. Her poems are fresh not simply because they are quite unlike anyone else's but because they seem to have appropriated a poetic speech and vocabulary hitherto unknown in American or English verse. She has a complete mastery of both sensuous and abstract words, and the success of her best lyrics is often due to a cunning juxtaposition of these two modes of language. She is one of the very few poets who can shock and delight as easily and directly by her handling of abstractions as by the justness and decorum of her concrete imagery. Let me give an example of what I mean by quoting one of her poems:

> Exultation is the going
> Of an inland soul to sea,
> Past the houses, past the headlands,
> Into deep eternity.
>
> Bred as we, among the mountains,
> Can the sailor understand
> The divine intoxication
> Of the first league out from land?

Death is the subject of many of Emily Dickinson's poems, and death for her is as near, as familiar, as commonplace even, as love affairs are in the poems of less self-sufficient poets. Yet she is not a domestic poet, nor a writer who has found a comfortable niche among matters and subjects which are usually thought to be the special province of women poets. Her poems are as bare as Emily Brontë's, as ecstatic as some of Blake's shorter lyrics. If her poems are short, if she is economical and extremely severe with herself, this is because her subjects are so large that they are more effectively presented, more resonant, if they are only hinted at rather than considered at length or extended into long meditations. Her visions are so elusive that to be truthful to them, to suggest the momentariness of their coming and going, she too must be

brief but also precise. So in the following twelve-line poem, she
tells us more about the questing, visionary mind than many
other poets have succeeded in doing in a complete *œuvre:*

> The soul selects her own society,
> Then shuts the door.
> To her divine majority
> Present no more.
>
> Unmoved she notes the chariots pausing
> At her low gate;
> Unmoved, an Emperor be kneeling
> Upon her mat.
>
> I've known her from an ample nation
> Choose one,
> Then close the valves of her attention
> Like stone.

Allen Tate has some useful things to say about this power of
Emily Dickinson's to ensnare and hold an elusive idea:

> It is a poetry of ideas [he says], and it demands of the
> reader a point of view—not an opinion of the New Deal
> or of the League of Nations, but an ingrained philosophy
> that is fundamental, a settled attitude that is almost
> extinct in this eclectic age. Yet it is not the sort of poetry
> of ideas which, like Pope's, requires a point of view only.
> It requires also, for the deepest understanding, which
> must go beneath the verbal excitement of the style, a
> highly developed sense of the specific quality of poetry—a
> quality that most persons accept as the accidental feature
> of something else that the poet thinks he has to say.

Thus Emily Dickinson's poems would seem to demand not only an open sympathy from the reader but also the deepest and most sensitive kind of poetic response. She asks for a total engagement, not necessarily a complete surrender but certainly an acquiescence of the mind and an alertness of the senses. As has been said already, this is a poet who extorted the largest possible amount of poetic material from the most apparently meager personal experience. The explanation of this phenomenon is, of course, that Emily Dickinson had an intensely rich inner life. One might almost say that what mountains were to Wordsworth and what social life was to Pope, the movements of her own mind and heart were to Emily Dickinson.

Elizabeth Jennings (b. 1926) has authored numerous books of criticism and poetry, including *Every Changing Shape* and her own *Collected Poems*.

...

INDEX